A NATION OF SERFS

How the Greatest Generation shackled us
with debt

By
BRYCE WEBSTER

Muffin Dog Press

ii

Published in 2013 by FeedARead.com Publishing – Arts Council funded as Eating Their Young by Bryce Webster.

Copyright © 2014 by Muffin Dog Press.

Copyright © 2015 by Muffin Dog Press.

A CIP catalogue record for this title is available from the British Library.

ISBN-13: 978-1500724719
ISBN-10: 1500724718

Visit the publisher's website at www.muffindogpress.com.

Muffin Dog Press

A Nation of Serfs

How the Greatest Generation shackled us with debt

TABLE OF CONTENTS

INTRODUCTION

While finishing this book, and having felt heavy inside for months, I read a quote variously attributed to St. Augustine and Nelson Mandela, and probably others. It reads:

Resentment is like drinking poison and hoping the other person dies.

It is certainly true that I resent, and am angry about, the treatment of my generation, first by our parents and the politicians they elected, and second by Tom Brokaw's disingenuous, but unfortunately persistent, lionizing of that generation as the greatest. It was nothing of the sort. No generation is the greatest. Not even the Baby Boom.

The problem for the Baby Boom is that, even before Brokaw rang in with his unexamined tripe, the Baby Boom had been vilified for decades, first (of course) by its own parents, and later by Generation X whose anger at the breadth and depth of the material on view (TV, radio, Internet, print) about the Baby Boom rankled. The sheer mass of Baby Boom information was, understandably, enough to make them feel as if the Baby Boom was the only generation that counted. Nor were many Baby Boomers able to accept anything about Generation X, anymore than the GI Generation had accepted anything about the Baby Boom, leading to more resentment. There will probably always be generational discord, much as there will always be poor people. Still, the obsession of the Greatest Generation with accruing to themselves all they could and more, and disdain for their own children and grandchildren, struck me as a bit excessive, even in the current age of excess.

As I explored the possible reasons for this inordinate interest in Boomer bashing by both its elders and younger generations, I found that, to put it in pop psychology terms, a generation that was making itself feel good by making others feel bad. The Greatest, underneath, was nothing of the sort and knew it. Their response to their perceptions of their own inadequacy, exacerbated by Tom Brokaw's disingenuous elevation of one generation above all others, has been devastating for Baby Boomers, and will be devastating for our children and our children's children.

Understanding why the over-reaching generation before us vilifies us is one thing. But why does the next generation, our children, and the one after that vilify the Boomers? Boomers invented the "precious child" syndrome, lavishing on our kids everything we could manage, from breastfeeding almost until Junior was ready to rent his Prom tux, to computers. A puzzlement.

But not really. We didn't have as much to give our kids as we would have liked, even though we had far fewer kids per family than our parents had. But we also had flat wages; our parents' generation's wages had risen consistently over their working lives. And we Boomers had ever-increasing FICA demands to pay for our parents, many of whom retired as our kids were born. We experienced ever-widening disparity between the well-off and the barely making it. As a result, we had more and more mothers working to try to counteract that; our kids didn't get home-made cookies, as we did. And perhaps we didn't give them all the nurturing they needed in other ways, either. We just gave them "stuff."

The Baby Boom has not always reacted perfectly to the perfect storm of parental greed by Brokaw's greatest, the demands of our own children and the government sloth we have encountered on our journey to and through adulthood. Worst of all, we allowed ourselves to be fragmented, to give up on our early promise that led to the end of Nixonian politics, the expansion of civil rights and gender rights, many successful interventions in environmental disaster, the ubiquitous PC, and more. To hear our parents tell it, we are a worthless and unsuccessful bunch. To hear our children tell it, we are an over-achieving bunch and too possessive of our success for anyone's good, particularly theirs.

What's the truth?

The truth is that the Baby Boom had a lot to contend with coming in. We were born into a generational and often familial litter, and into a stultified world in which sexism and racism were accepted as normal. We had the Cold War. Remember tucking your head between your knees — under your desk — and kissing your ass goodbye? It was truly frightening to most of us, and we had nightmares about it. It was frightening when your parents shopped for a new house complete with bomb shelter, which we intrinsically knew was worthless, but was supposed to protect us, stocked with canned goods and Saltine crackers, for six months while we waited for nuclear winter to subside. We had overcrowded classrooms, overcrowded colleges we had to fight and claw to get into, and then had to pay for ourselves. We had an endless war we were castigated for loathing, but one for which our young men volunteered at a greater rate than the so-called heroes in our parents' generation volunteered for WWII, the war they and Brokaw claim made them the greatest.

Our first presidential election gave us a choice of Republican Richard M. Nixon, Democrat Hubert Humphrey, segregationist/American Independent Party candidate George Wallace...or comedian Dick Gregory as a write-in candidate. I wrote in Gregory. And I will never know whether all of us who did, in a fit of pique at a weak Democrat or a criminal Republican or an execrable throwback to an age most of us hoped was gone, stole the election from Humphrey.

There was, and is, a lot on our plate. More than any other generation? Arguably, except X and Y, who will somehow have to shoulder a large burden after years of shouldering relatively little. Relatively. They have had their war. Two wars, if you will, and wildly unpopular ones in some of the United States and most of the rest of the world. And the maiming of soldiers in them has been horrific. The wars were started by George W. Bush, by birth year, a Boomer. But not, I submit, under any other rubric. Bush is a perpetual adolescent, whereas most Boomers — the ones not coddled by one of the world's richest families — grew up right quick. Still, Bush has provided a disastrous presidency on the basis of which generations X and Y would have to be perspicacious indeed not to resent us. We must forgive them. We can best do that, I think, by refusing to accept Bush as one of us...by, in effect, exiling him from a generation he does not deserve to belong to. Indeed, he was, in any case, simply the lackey of Silent Generation member Dick Cheney, and the approval-seeking least son of GI Generation's George H.W. Bush.

I realize that sounds tawdry, trying to shift a Boomer out of the cohort lest the cohort be tarnished. But actually, it seems eminently sensible. Some in the GI Generation would certainly disavow Richard M. Nixon, a masterfully arrogant and generally abhorred president who escaped impeachment and conviction by the skin of his teeth, one of theirs by birth.

***

I wrote this book not to excuse the Baby Boom for either its failures or its successes, but to point out the factors that led to the situation in which the Baby Boom generation finds itself; maxed out by the government that gave its parents everything, and looking at a future so bleak, especially compared to the last decades of the GI Generation, that it will be a wonder if suicide doesn't become the greatest cause of death among older Boomers.

World's largest generation has world's highest suicide rate

It is, in fact, an increasing factor in Baby Boom mortality. In 2008, Alan L. Berman, executive director of the American Association of Suicidology, said that the suicide rate among older people was decreasing. He was quoted in *US News & World Report*, saying, "We don't know any more about that than we do about the increase among middle-aged people. We are always concerned about understanding these kinds of trends, but they need to go on for many years in order to truly define them as something significant and different." (Reinberg 2008)

Berman thought that the increased rate was the "Baby Boomer explanation." Since the generation was large, one would expect to see a greater number of suicides than in previous generations. His simplistic claim is without merit. It was the percentage of suicides in the middle-aged population, not the sheer number of them; of course there would be numerically more in the larger population than in the smaller, even if the percentage was constant. It was not.

Here's a clue to the discrepancy. By October, 2008, middle-aged people — Baby Boomers — had no hope of a decent old age. At the moment Berman was quoted, Boomers — the middle-aged — had seen such meager pensions as they had amassed decrease by 40 percent or more, their houses devalued by as great a percentage, and their obligations increasing as the parents they cared for got more feeble, and the children who had been out spending like there was no tomorrow moved back home.

The study on which the article was based took place between 1999 and 2005, however, meaning Boomer suicide rates were already rising before the magnitude of Bush's perfidy came to light. It was a trend while the only factors known to be extant were those wrought by previous, anti-citizen presidents, notably Reagan and Bush I. Boomers have somewhat accurately been called the best-educated generation ever; no doubt, if that is only partly true, they could see the writing on the wall and became hopeless.

A year after the study to which Berman was responding, another study noted that, "Boomers 45 to 64 have the highest suicide rate of all age groups..." according to information form the National Center for Health Statistics and provided by Dr. Myrna Weissman, a Columbia University psychiatry professor speaking for an article in the *New York Times*.

"It's the economy, stupid." For Clinton, and for every Boomer

According to the federal Suicide Prevention Resource Center's website, suicide is linked to unemployment. Author Michael Winerip noted that, "The economy is an A-1 stressor." Or, as First Boomer President often — and apparently correctly — said, "It's the economy, stupid."

Mr. Bush was apparently stupid. He was not a Rhodes scholar and lawyer, like Mr. Clinton. He was a completely forgettable, pushed-through-for-Daddy Yale MBA with a degree bought and paid for, not earned and appreciated. Mr. Bush was too ignorant even to latch onto Mr. Clinton's prescription, or too greedy. I would submit that both apply.

In addition, Mr. Bush's excesses (although they might better be called deficiencies) have opened the Baby Boom up to even more undeserved bashing than it has gotten the past few years, in the virtual cottage industry that has grown up around Boomer Bashing.[1]

***

This book may well anger people. I fully expect it to anger the GI Generation. But, like George W. Bush, that most reprehensible example of the Boomer generation (although a member by chronology only), the GI Generation may choose to

---

[1] "I'm getting seriously tired of 'Pin-the-Tail-on-the-Boomers' particulary this tendency to make ludicrously broad generalizations about 70 million people born over the course of almost 30 years. Four separate cohorts. I take particular exception to being blamed for trends which date back to the previous generation – the Boomers' parents. And laws passed when they were in charge as well." *Cynthia Shepherd* (Norris, 2006)

stick its head in the ground, glossing over the greed and cupidity it has exhibited for fifty years.

I am hoping the Baby Boom generation is angered to the point that, at last, we will demand a change in leadership, a real change. Not change we can believe in, but change that has proven its worth so that believing will not be a matter of faith, but a matter of observation. Mr. Obama may well be able to deliver that change, if the bloated minions of the GI Generation ever decided to get out of his way. But if not him, then we must make it happen somehow, and soon.

First, though, we need to understand that the Greatest Generation is great in only one measure: The way they set up their children, and all the generations after, for an Epic Fail.

DEFINITIONS

Although a few sources use either earlier or later starting dates, the most common definition of the Baby Boom includes children born between 1946 and 1964. This is the most logical delineation because it encompasses the returning warfighters and leaves an 18-year window in which to create families.

A working definition of the Silent Generation includes those people born between 1923 and 1945. This was the generation raised as the Depression was winding down, and whose young men never experienced a major or protracted war. They were too young to be drafted for WWII, and some were too young for Korea. There were a few that served in Korea, alongside some WWII veterans. But the conflict was not long enough or fierce enough, and did not consume sufficient members of the cohort to become defining, as Vietnam was for the Baby Boom and WWII was for the GI Generation, later misnamed the Greatest Generation by Silent Generation cohort member Tom Brokaw.

The GI Generation is that born between 1901 and 1922. Those born in the teens probably constituted most of the GIs; those born before 1910 or so would have been too old for the draft in 1940. While the generation claims that their service in WWII defines it, they also lay claim to being defined by the Great Depression; however, there is a fallacy in that claim. As children, they might have been affected by the Depression, but did not have to struggle with it as their parents, born before the turn of the century, did.

CHAPTER ONE:
THE SETTING FOR THE FEAST, OR THE
PALPABLE GREED TABLEAU

It is unfortunate that Tom Brokaw, formerly a news reader for a major network, chose to go all weepy and mushy over a generation of American men and women who had already placed themselves in the untenable position of being the parents of the largest generation ever born. These self-proclaimed Great Depression children (they're not; their parents bore the brunt of that), nonetheless had so much faith in America and so much faith in themselves that they thought nothing of having more babies in a shorter time span than any other generation in history. This despite the tales of deprivation they liked to regale the Baby Boom with, despite the fact that when they went to war, they were young men hard-pressed to find good employment as they finally came of age at the tail end of the Depression. At the very least, they would seem to have exercised poor judgment; at the worst, selfishness the like of which the world had never seen before.

WWII Generation equals cocaine-crazed hookers

The WWII generation that Brokaw has elevated on an apparently unscalable pedestal was either the worst bunch of Pollyannas ever to grace the landscape, or it got hooked early on government largesse unique in history. It would seem the latter possibility is closer to the truth. Once hooked — like cocaine-crazed prostitutes — they went to extraordinary lengths to avoid giving up so much as a single grain of the goodies they had been shooting up since they came marching home.

A frequent libertarian contributor to the national debate, blogger Russell Madden, has identified a great many of the excesses of the WWII generation. Among those he offers are these:

- The 'Greatest Generation' clamored for loans and subsidies and special favors that breed political corruption, civilian cynicism, and that reward the inefficient at the expense of the capable.
- The 'Greatest Generation' stood at the helm of a 'Great Society' that declared a 'War on Poverty' and created a growing underclass of poor people.
- The 'Greatest Generation' decided to wage a 'War on Drugs' that is eviscerating the Constitution they swore to defend while it fills our prisons with nonviolent 'criminals' and undermines the integrity of law-enforcement personnel.
- The 'Greatest Generation' sent our troops to Korea and Vietnam, to the Arabian Gulf and NATO Europe, and to Africa and South America, helping set in motion the animosity that culminated in the attacks of 9-11-01. (Madden blog)

The so-called Greatest Generation is the one that can also be credited with:

- Neglecting to provide for their children's educations except by saddling those children with loans which, despite the dearth of jobs for Boomers, would eventually be made non-dischargeable in bankruptcy;
- Expanding Social Security for themselves, and then ensuring that their children would be impoverished to pay for the wealth transfer as the older members of

Congress voted for cost-of-living adjustments that far outstripped the raises working people could expect;

- Creating Medicare, a very expensive addition to the wealth transfer from the Boomers and Generation X, Y and beyond to the older folks; and,

- Creating a war especially for Baby Boomers, Vietnam, that had nothing whatever to do with American safety, or even American needs for oil, sending their sons there, and then refusing to give them what they needed to win the war, not to mention making the decision to pull out when so many of those sons had been sacrificed for nothing and then telling the kids they were not much at fighting, all the while tossing into jails or sending the National Guard in against those sons and daughters who objected to the useless war.

Correction: Not useless. It cut down on the procreation possibilities of the Boomer Generation both by death and by the understandable reluctance of many of that generation to bring children into the world they knew. Their father's world. The world created for the so-called Greatest Generation by its own generous WWI-veteran fathers, and a world which the insatiably greedy World War II generation would remake to its own service and enrichment at the expense of virtually everyone else for generations to come.

"The U.S. economy speeds toward a brick wall. But instead of trying to stop or even slow the fiscal train wreck, many senior citizens want to push hard on the accelerator.

"Nothing was more evident at the recent 2005 White House Conference on Aging than the palpable greed of seniors. Perhaps they see it as getting even with their Baby Boomer kids for how we aggravated them in the 1960s and '70s."(*Washington Times* 2005)

The death of the elderly, and the birth of the senior citizen

Adding insult to injury, that generation decided they didn't want to be called old people; they wanted to be senior citizens. By inference, then, everyone else is a junior citizen. Few people like to spend their lives being "junior" in anything, especially if they have worked and struggled like everyone else on the planet.

It would be news to the WWII Generation, not long on making the fine distinction between honesty and appearance, but accolades cannot be demanded; they can only be deserved.

The Greatest? Only Muhammad Ali in recent history

Whenever a person claims greatness for herself, isn't there a justified hint of suspicion that they are, in fact, not the greatest? Muhammad Ali claimed to be the greatest, though, and he really was in the single thing he claimed to be the greatest in. Perhaps that's what confused people on that issue. But it needn't have. He knew himself, and realized not only that he had the talent, but also the will to be great.

In the case of the Greatest Generation, they have simply appropriated a title that is too broad, in fact, to be meaningful, but makes them feel good while, by contrast and inference, making everyone else feel bad. It is bogus *a priori*. They did not achieve it, but were granted it by someone who was busy plowing his own field of fame and fortune and, if truth be told, might be considered to have used that generation as fodder for his own mill.

Does Brokaw think the Founding Fathers are chopped liver?

Does Brokaw really believe they are the single greatest generation in history? If he does, he didn't even deserve to be a talking head, being ignorant of the American generation that wrote a new political book for mankind, the Founding Fathers. Being ignorant of the artist/scientists of Venice during the Renaissance who opened up the universe for us, often at the cost of their lives. Being ignorant of the philosophers of ancient Greece, who gave us the idea to think about living and dying. In fact, there is no single greatest generation in history, American or other.

But, just in case you are not yet convinced that the so-called Greatest Generation was actually rather ordinary when it wasn't being foolhardy or reckless, here are some cogent questions to ask regarding the true greatness of the Greatest Generation, raised at one time or another in many blogs, but perhaps notably on the TwelveAngryMen blog:

- Whatever your opinion of the reasons for the Vietnam War, its management was execrable. Why, since Boomers were young adults or children at the time is the Boomer generation blamed for it? The decision makers, who are properly to blame, were the World War II generation.

- Who was in charge during the 1970s when stagflation was destroying   jobs and lives, and during the next decade? Not the Boomers.

- Who presided over the sudden deification of the old over the young during the 1960s and 1970s, leading to the giant expenditures for and shortfalls in "entitlement programs" such as Social Security?

- Whose programs gutted inner cities, leaving rat playgrounds where nice little neighborhoods had once been, or creating Soviet-style high rises as replacements for human-scale houses and apartment blocks? (TwelveAngryMen blog 2005)

It is difficult to credit how a generation that truly was the greatest at anything could be so completely responsible for the despicable juggernauts above.

Clearly, they can't claim greatness based on these blunders. But what about the war itself, the war that helped Brokaw create the undeserved cache? Were they the greatest then?

The "Greatest" were more like World War II duds than Scuds

A brothersjudd review of Brokaw's book indicates that the answer is resoundingly no. Among other things, the review asks:

- How difficult a task was it to win WWII? With Japan failing miserably in its desperate gamble at Pearl Harbor and the German offensive grinding to a halt in Russia, was there any way that we could have failed to win the war or wasn't this merely a mopping up operation, however costly?

- Having freed half of Europe, why did this generation abandon the Eastern half of the continent to the ministrations of Stalin and the USSR? Do the dead of the gulag really feel comforted by the fact that America allowed them to be murdered by Stalin and not Hitler?

- Did this generation's responsibilities cease on V-J Day? Besides the question of the Soviet Union, where was this generation during the Cold War, Korea, Vietnam, etc? Were they responsible for these failures or merely unsupportive of our soldiers during them?

- Do the difficulties of the Depression and service in WWII really justify the massive transfer of payments that this generation has secured to themselves from future generations? Social Security, Medicare, etc. are justly called entitlements; why is this generation the one in our history that felt entitled to so much in exchange for their service to the nation?

- Do they bear no responsibility for the enormous deficits that were rung up throughout their lifetimes, in order to pay for the thorough Social Safety Net they demanded? Deficits, mind you, which our generation will be the one to pay off over the next twenty or thirty years."(CSPAN booknotes 2009)

The brothersjudd website does misappropriate some responsibility, however. Those who would debunk the Greatest Generation myth ask:

- If there really was a horrible darkness falling on Europe and this generation fought it out of a sense of duty, why did they stay out of the fight for a full two years, until the Japanese attacked us?, and,
- Why did they declare war only on Japan at that point, waiting until Hitler declared war on us to return the favor?"(CSPAN booknotes 2009)

WWII Generation members also claim that their horrific experiences during World War II entitle them to the appellation the Greatest Generation. Really? They saw a fraction of the battle time experienced by Vietnamese troops; WWII troops saw an average of 40 days of battle spread over four years, while US troops in Vietnam saw 240 days EVERY year. (McCaffrey 1993)

The Vietnam Helicopter Flight Crew Network website noted that, "One out of every 10 Americans who served in Vietnam was a casualty. 58,169 were killed and 304,000 wounded out of 2.59 million who served. Although the percent who died is similar to other wars, amputations or crippling wounds were 300 percent higher than in World War II. 75,000 Vietnam veterans are severely disabled." (VHFCN 2009)

Brokaw doesn't even have greater amounts or greater depth of service on which to base his unreasoned and unreasonable accolades.

WWII vets dodged the draft in much greater percentages than Vietnam vets

Nor will bravery or patriotism put the WWII vets over the top as compared to Vietnam vets. In a speech in Washington DC in 1986, Gen. William C. Westmoreland noted that 2/3 of those who served in Vietnam were volunteers, whereas 2/3 of those who served in WWII were drafted. Adding to the debunking of the WWII patriotism myth, McCaffrey noted that during Vietnam, many volunteered for the draft, so that even some of the nominal draftees were in fact volunteers. (Westmoreland 1986)

The brothersjudd author is guilty with those two questions, however, of doing precisely what he accuses the WWII generation of doing to the Baby Boom. The WWII generation was not responsible for staying out of WWII: that was THEIR fathers' decision. They are guilty of much, but not of that.

The brothersjudd website author also notes that the Baby Boom might be the most coddled generation ever to walk the earth, but also asks, who raised them? It is highly likely, however, that the Baby Boom is not nearly as spoiled as the World War II generation would paint them...anymore than Baby Boomer soldiers were as cowardly as they were painted by the World War II generation; just the opposite considering they served more days under worse conditions than any WWII vet did.

Besides that, the Baby Boom is taking care of its parents, both via the transfer payments that are Social Security and Medicare, by cash donations from their own pockets, and by doing without the "grandpa" assistance their own parents enjoyed while raising their kids — because the Baby Boom's kids' grandpas are off in Sun City, enjoying their locked-in transfer payments, i.e., Social Security, and fully vested pensions. Meanwhile, the Boomers worry about how they will ever retire, what with the enormous demands on their resources, including:

- The sums going out for transfer payments such as Social Security and Medicare
- Supplemental help so their WWII Generation parents need never miss a vacation
- Costs, both direct and indirect, for the care of parents unable to care for themselves
- Education for their own children, and,
- Recouping the 40 percent of what little they had managed to save for retirement that was wiped out by the Bush recession.[2]

Add to all that the fact that the WWII Generation was the very last one to get defined benefit retirement plans, and it's a miracle Boomers haven't once again manned the ramparts and demanded change, as they so effectively did during the Vietnam War.

As for Brokaw's chosen few: Are they the Greatest Generation? Hardly. The term Greediest comes immediately to mind.

---

[2] While corporations funded pensions for the WWII Generation, when it came time for the Baby Boom to become vested in retirement plans, the WWII the Greediest had dumped corporate pensions and instituted IRAs and Keoghs, pushing the entire burden for retirement onto the Boomers' own shoulders, at the very time those Boomers were trying to raise children in a stagnant 1970s economy, and paying ever-increasing taxes for Social Security to fund the WWII the Greediest' retirement. Nothing changes. This will be dealt with in more depth in later chapters. Suffice it to say that when the average American wage is under $35,000 per year, castigating people for not saving more is stupid at best, cruel at worst—and yet, both of those are facts of Baby Boom life at the hands of the so-called Greatest Generation.

I am hardly alone in regarding Brokaw's term as misused and misplaced. The late Howard Zinn, Professor of Political Science at Boston University, author, historian and activist, was a bombardier during WWII and should, therefore, have reveled in being a member of the Greatest Generation.

In fact, he reviled the term. Zinn wrote, "I refuse to celebrate them as 'the greatest generation' because in doing so we are celebrating courage and sacrifice in the cause of war. And we are miseducating the young to believe that military heroism is the noblest form of heroism, when it should be remembered only as the tragic accompaniment of horrendous policies driven by power and profit."(Zinn 2001)

CHAPTER TWO:
EDUCATION, THE GIFT THE GI
GENERATION USED AND ABUSED

Why did the population of the United States have such a hard time understanding universal health insurance in 2009 and 2010? And why are people both older and younger than the Boomers terrified of socialism and, at the same time, totalitarianism? Look no farther than what has happened to American education.

Granted, there are Boomers whose education leaves much to be desired. But the numbers of the Greediest and the post-Boomers who have not the slightest inkling of history, economics, or culture and who have not the foggiest idea of how to analyze a problem logically, not to mention applying logic in a humanitarian way, point to a serious lack of education as the problem. And it is a problem that started before the Boomers came along, but was exacerbated ten-fold by Greeder Wannabe Bush with his No Child Left Behind (NCLB) program; more on that later.

What is missing is in America is real education, classical university education which encompasses at least a smattering of the great thoughts of humankind. This is not the trade school sort of education that got its start after World War II, was refined further for the Baby Boom, and has by now reduced education to ineffectual mind games, from No Child Left Behind in the public school classroom, to colleges dismissing professors who dare to utter a non-politically correct thought. (Or to Liberty University, if one wants a stellar answer to the question, "When is a college not a college?" While the

University of Phoenix is probably as incestuous as Liberty U., and probably has even less claim to a higher education title of any sort, Liberty University's right-wing religious fundamentalism defines it as a trade school for Jesus freaks rather than any sort of bona fide institution of higher learning.)

The Yanks and Brits may speak the same language, but tests prove Brits speak it better

In 2007, Great Britain had racked up 25 years of improving grades on its standardized tests. In the United States, during the same period, scores on its major standardized test, the Scholastic Aptitude Test (SAT), declined. However, this has been explained away by the fact that more lower-income people of all ethnic groups had begun to take the test and that their scores had climbed each year. So, while their addition to the ranks of test-takers had swelled and thereby diluted the better scores of more affluent whites, overall, scores were on the way up, some argue.

But the author of a study of the phenomena associated with educational test scores cites evidence that scoring of tests in the US became more *lenient* during this time, substantially belaying any "waffle room" the expansion of the testing population might have provided. He notes that, "Denying a 19-year decline is the educational equivalent of denying that smoking causes lung cancer."(Dutch 2010)

What killed off Baby Boomers' test scores? Their parents. Their parents who entered college not because they had the funds and the previous education to do so, as their parents' generation had had to do. Their parents who didn't even have to sit for the Scholastic Aptitude Test (SAT) for college entrance. Their parents who, with arguably inadequate preparation, were admitted to colleges with very little discernment on the part of college admissions personnel; being a GI was just about enough for admission just about anywhere. Boomer's parents, a generation that was, despite increasing college experience, ill-educated and ill-prepared, became their teachers.

Education had been expanded wildly for the Greediest Generation by the generation before. That WWI generation — the fathers of the GIs, also sometimes called the Lost Generation — well recalled the riots after WWI vets came home and could find no jobs. They reasoned that sending the WWII vets to college would allow the economy some time to adjust to their return, and ultimately provide the former soldiers with jobs. The Greediest — those same soldiers who mopped up in Europe but took full credit for defeating Hitler almost single-handedly (never mind the Russians who whacked Hitler's eastern front and Hitler's own overextension) took full advantage of the expansion in educational opportunities and a marvelous free ride, out of the care of the US military, and into the care of captains of industry with nary a pause for breath.

GIs' children, many of whom had served in Vietnam with distinction in a much more rigorous theater, came to expect the same opportunities. The scenario for them was, however, far different than it had been for their fathers. Not only was their ride on a rickety bus; their destination would not be not solid jobs with good pay and benefits, but a scramble for anything available after graduation.

WWII made grunts into putative geniuses…as long as someone else paid the bills

The authors of the GI Bill had expected the returning GIs to do trade-school sorts of programs such as business management. But the GIs preferred liberal arts. Fortunately for the GIs, industry — having ramped up for the war effort — was eager for any educated employee, so going into banking with a degree in philology was not unheard of. Becoming a teacher was easier still.

It must be mentioned that while the GIs headed for college wanted liberal arts degrees and not professional ones, a large number of GIs used the GI Bill for various sorts of trade schools. Two and a half times as many GIs as went to college used the benefit for sub-college training, including "3.5 million in public and for-profit schools; 1.4 million in non-agricultural on-the-job training; and 700,000 in on-the-farm training—5.6 million veterans in all, more than a third of the men and women who had served in the war…." (Altschuler and Blumin 2009)

The Baby Boomers didn't have it so good. They, too, sought a classical education, although often encouraged to study something practical. (Are the voices in your head replaying Archie Bunker berating Meathead for studying political science instead of business management?) As the first Boomers graduated from college, the economy was not growing sufficiently to permit possession of a liberal arts degree to get them into a profitable career. The ability to use the benefits for the wide range of other education the Greediest enjoyed was curtailed and, in any case, during the first wave of Boomer industrial employment, the Greediest moved to destroy the unions that protected those wages.

Nor was that the worst of it. The dilution of education was bad enough for Boomers. For Boomers' children, not only has the economy shut down, the Boomer's kids and kids' kids won't even have the solace of a reasonably good education and the ability to think, as the downward slide that inevitably began with Boomer classroom overcrowding culminated in the political correctness (i.e., sanctions against intellectual curiosity) of colleges today, and in the most execrable educational program ever devised by mankind, No Child Left Behind.

When does Walter Mitty become a genius?

By now — beginning with the steep downward slide that began when all the WWII grunts began imagining themselves to be Immanuel Kant but actually bringing their Walter Mitty selves to the workplace — education virtually does not exist.

But in America, always willing to don the rose-colored glasses, the illusion persists.

Angela Hoy, an ethical woman who runs the very valuable website for writers, *Writer's Weekly*, is adamantly opposed to the paper mills that provide term papers for a price and even doctoral dissertations for university students. She regards paper mills as unethical on every possible front.

While I admire Ms. Hoy and all she does, I respectfully disagree on that point; the existence and use of paper mills is ethically neutral in the new world of what passes for American education. When an intelligent young woman I know well could consider getting her degree from the University of Phoenix, something is wrong. When she thought that way because an old friend of her late mother was both a product of and teacher at the University of Phoenix (BA and MA) — and who moreover thought paper mills to be the work of the devil while the University of Phoenix provided an education — something is very seriously wrong.

Fortunately, that young woman, being intelligent, saw the truth in time and went to a real college for a real degree. But the greater tragedy is this: American education, after all the post-War years of dumbing it down, is no longer academia. It is a profit-based credentialing system which has nothing to do with the great thoughts of mankind, and everything to do with how students can get an employer to see that student as the best of the crop, hire that student, and apply large doses of both stultifying overwork and unconscionable overpayment to that hireling.   (This is true least in some circles, while others can't get jobs flipping burgers in the 2010 economy.) In such a culture, then, it would seem not only expedient, but enterprising and smart, for so-called scholars to pay term paper mills to raise their credentials above those of the crowd. Indeed, it would seem that only a stupid student, or one who had acquired some *bona fide* education someplace other than US public schools (itself a miracle), would not do so. A preponderance of badly prepared students would seem, in the wake of NCLB, to be far more likely than a preponderance of educated students.

Education judged by the number of footnotes

And indeed, that seems to be the case. Writer Nick Mamatas, a novelist, filled in spare time and plumped his bank account for a time by writing term papers. The gig gave him an insight into why students can't write term papers; they've never seen one. What they are asked to read in school is far more like chick lit than the great books of the world. They never experience factual works with footnotes, or at least, in-text citations. They never dissect arguments, nor are they encouraged to make their own arguments, supported by the thoughts of others. Perhaps that's the wages of the textbook industry, whereby students are provided with anthologies of bowdlerized works, often denuded of anything that the school boards in Texas, a major purchaser of school texts and thus influential to publishers who then sell the texts elsewhere, might consider supportive of evolution or other concepts the fundamentalists find dangerous. Recently, the Texas school board revised its curriculum based on conservative ideologies. Among other things:

> Cynthia Dunbar, a lawyer from Richmond who is a strict constitutionalist and thinks the nation was founded on Christian beliefs, managed to cut Thomas Jefferson from a list of figures whose writings inspired revolutions in the late 18th century and 19th century, replacing him with St. Thomas Aquinas, John Calvin and William Blackstone. (Jefferson is not well liked among conservatives on the board because he coined the term 'separation between church and state.') (McKinley 2010)

Mamatas found reasons to excuse some purchasers of term papers. Think, he said, of a poetry major taking required chemistry. Or vice versa. (Another argument, and one Mamatas makes, for the European style of "reading" a subject, as is done at Oxford.)

Other purchasers were foreign nationals and often professionals who had to repeat their degrees in English, because unaccountably the US regards other nations' educational systems as inferior.

Some were just lazy.

But the vast majority, he claims, were just uneducated dolts, relieving him of the necessity of feeling too bad about taking their money. Indeed, such students are "being cheated by the schools that take tuition and give nothing in exchange [such as the U. of Phoenix, one might argue]."(Mamatas 2010)

Mamatas offers verbatim his instructions from one such client:

> i need you to write me two different story in all these listed under. The introduction of the story, the themes, topic and character, please not from internet, Or any posted web sites, because my professor will know if from internet this is the reason why i' m spending money on it.Not two much words, because i will still write it back in clsss go straight to the point and write me the conclution at end of the two story, the second story different introduction, themes, topic and character. Thank you God Bless.

Mamatas concluded, "At the parties I go to, people start off laughing, but then they stop."

***

Does that beg the ethics of it all? One can posit a number of assumptions and arrive at the conclusion that paper mills are, at worst, neither ethical nor unethical for either the students or the writers, or certainly for the companies that create the match.

Submitted:

1. Education has been on a slide toward the trade-school level since the GIs returned and demanded, without benefit of the classics studied by university students gone before, to be given a university education, if in name only.

2. The downward slide continued, exacerbated by a slowing of the capitalist-industrialist economic engine that necessarily accompanied the invention of machines, and eventually computers, that hastened the death of hand work of any sort.

3. The arrival of the Internet put paid to the publishing industry; reading and even studying books for the bulk of those in industrial societies who would have had to read in earlier times, if only instruction manuals for their trade, became unnecessary. The ubiquitous hand-helds made it possible for mind-numbed millions to play computer games at the bus stop, rather than read a newspaper as they might have done in the past.

4. The first three factors (and doubtless more) created a population unused to reading, never mind researching and putting two coherent thoughts together on paper. It also created a generation of writers, mainly Boomers and Gen Xers, starving to death. The more extensively the Internet permeated life, the less need there was for writers; information was disposable, literally. Nor was anyone rushing to hire writers for other jobs. Why? Because they could think. And thinking is precisely what employers do not, in the main, require these days. (An educated slave is a troublesome slave.)

Concluded:

What companies now require is credentialing, the pieces of paper that say an employee is capable of doing X job (or maybe

X and Y jobs, if he or she possesses a "skill set.") It would seem, then, that the term paper mill is a win-win-win situation. Here's how that works out:

- The writers get to earn an income at something they can actually do and enjoy;
- The students get their credentials, and the students more willing to hire really good paper mills get better credentials still, and;
- The employers get the trained apes they want.

In addition, a few members of the current generation of graduates get jobs, thereby avoiding standing on what was predicted to be, in 2010, a decade-long unemployment line.

In the current universe — not some dream landscape that was hastened away in about 1950 after lingering for a century — term paper purchase is ethically neutral.

But to begin at the beginning....

The root of the downfall of American education: The GI Bill

The single piece of legislation that can be credited with the downhill slide of American education is the GI Bill, also known as the Servicemen's Readjustment Act. It would not be hyperbole to refer to the GI Bill as the most extensive support program for education ever devised in human history. Although Congressional conservatives wanted to limit the bill to helping returning soldiers adjust to life after the battlefields of World War II, liberals viewed it as a means for social engineering to play a major role in the future of the nation. Indeed, within a year and a half of the bill's signing, it had been expanded from a temporary safety net into a way to help returning GIs realize their long-term ambitions. As Altschuler and Blumin note, "the GI Bill carried the New Deal into the post-war period under the cover of a veteran's benefit package and gave new legitimacy to the kinds of domestic programs enacted during the 1930s."(Altschuler and Blumin 2009, 7)

It also gave a significant leg up, not only in education but in housing, to the largest cohort of demobbed military in U.S. history. In 1955, there were 15,750,000 WWII veterans in civilian life.

A decade post-war, 78 percent of those had taken advantage of one or more of the three major benefits of the GI Bill.

By 1955:

- 8.3 million (52 percent) had received unemployment benefits, called "readjustment allowances"
- 7.8 million (just under half) had received college, graduate school, or job training benefits
- 4 million (25 percent) were granted VA-guaranteed loans for homes, farms or businesses. (Altschuler and Blumin 2009, 7)

Altschuler and Blumin note that of those who did not receive benefits, many were older and had already completed their education and had employment to return to, and did not need the benefits.

The GI Bill, according to Altschuler and Blumin, added to the nation's cadre of professionals:

450,000 engineers

180,000 doctors, dentists and nurses

360,000 teachers

150,000 scientists

243,000 accountants

107,000 lawyers

36,000 clergymen (2009, 86)

Moreover, although most of the benefits were used by white males, nonetheless, the GI Bill "clearly sustained post-war prosperity, fueled a revolution in rising expectations, and accelerated the shift to the post-industrial information age." (Olson 1974, 109)

An auxiliary benefit provided by the GI Bill supported an existing program, the VA hospitals. Many injured GIs benefited from medical care they might not have received without those hospitals nationwide, nor especially without the expansion of those hospitals under the GI Bill. The GI Bill provided funds for constructing medical facilities for GIs, and further stipulated that those hospitals would have access to scarce building materials on the same basis as did military bases. (Altschuler and Blumin 2009, 9)

The Greediest got used to the very best of a welfare state early and often

Returning WWII military personnel were being given the keys to the city, *en masse*. They received "readjustment allowances" for their living expenses, educational allowances and a virtually guaranteed loan for housing or to begin a business. No generation before or since has received anything even remotely akin to this largesse. Yet, today, it is the Greediest who are most vocal about the sub-prime mortgages and how lazy the young people are who applied for them and got them.

One wonders how many of the GIs would have been eligible for standard bank loans, especially as the job situation when they left for war was dire and many, many, many would not have had savings sufficient to buy homes. Indeed, without the GI Bill, it is reasonable to believe that the sub-prime meltdown, or something very similar, would have happened when the Greediest Generation was in its early earning years...had anyone in their father's generation or the Silent Generation had the greed to invent the sub-prime market, as the Greediest did for (to) the Boomers.

(No, Virginia, the Boomers did not invent the sub-prime market; look to the colleagues of Angelo R. Mozilo, CEO of Countrywide, to assess that cohort. Mozilo was born in 1938, into the immensely protected Silent Generation, and was too young or too old for virtually all recent wars. In addition, such a small cohort could more or less write its own ticket. Between Mozilo types and hyperbole-mavens like Brokaw, write it they did, to the detriment of everyone who came after.)

Under the GI Bill, as late as the 1970s, it was possible to buy a substantial home with no more than $500 out of one's pocket: I know, because I had married a recently demobbed Army officer and we took full advantage of the VA loan to buy our first house in 1970. And yes, we made money on it when we sold it less than a year later, but that was virtually the last housing profit for either of us. After that, the Vietnam action began winding down, GI benefits got scarcer, and the Nixon recession was looming...followed by several disastrous presidencies and the rise of the ruling financial oligarchy.

Luxury housing for Greediest college students

After World War II, those who were not ready to buy a home, having decided to go to college first, also needed a place to live, especially as such a vast number of the cohort married upon their return and started families almost immediately. Fortunately for them, Congress helped when the VA refused to help. Via the Lanham Act of 1940, Congress had authorized the federal government to construct public housing to facilitate the nation's defense. In response to the sudden urgent need for 47,300 single rooms and 22,120 apartments close to college campuses, Congress authorized the "National Housing Agency to rent housing to veterans, construct temporary units for them, move facilities to sites approved by colleges and universities, and reimburse institutions that had already incurred expenses in doing so. Congress appropriated almost $450,000,000 for these initiatives. When the funds ran out in August 1946, 101,462 accommodations had been transferred to institutions of higher education."(Altschuler and Blumin 2009, 88)

During the post-war years, Cornell University leased the Glen Springs Hotel in Watkins Glen, a lovely resort town at the southern end of Seneca Lake, one of New York's Finger Lakes. Cornell converted the hotel into apartments for 135 married veterans, and added "an infirmary, a sun porch, and a recreation lounge for dancing. Meals were served in a cafeteria set up in the main dining room" (Altschuler and Blumin 2009, 88) and the college bused students to the campus in Ithaca, a round trip of more than 50 miles. In the 1930s, the WPA had built a trail of stone walks and staircases along the gorge at Watkins Glen to the lake, complete with 19 charming waterfalls, providing an extraordinary leisure activity for the area and of course for the GI students and their growing families.

The contrast between the relative luxury to which parents of the Greediest treated their offspring and the penury in which so many Boomer college students scrabbled their way through college is stunning.

When the Baby Boom went to college, overcrowding was the norm, and there was no National Housing Agency to solve the problem. Three students were housed in rooms meant for two at virtually every public college and university, until some of the students dropped out, or failed, not unheard of since college classrooms were just as cut-throat from the overcrowding as public school classrooms had been. In the Boomer era, college cafeteria food was almost inedible, and recreation consisted of dorm dances in which the students themselves cleared furniture from the common room. Recreation lounge for dancing? Not likely. Free bus to class from a converted resort hotel as housing? Even less likely. Amenities like Watkins Glen with buses back and forth? No answer needed.

Harpur College, classical liberal arts school for WWII grunts

Cornell had also set up an outlying college, in Binghamton, NY. Housed in old residences and Quonset huts, Tri-Cities College became Harpur College a few years after it was founded using visiting Cornell faculty to serve GIs in the southern tier of New York State. Eventually, it was subsumed under the umbrella of the State University of New York, but it had benefitted greatly from its early association with a school of Cornell's caliber, and doubtless helped in the expansion of both IBM, located in nearby Endicott, NY, and Singer/Link technology company. In short, the educational plant made significant contributions to the local economy, one that had been predicated upon an older smokestack industry paradigm before the Depression struck.

However, as the years passed, SUNY Binghamton became Binghamton University, still a part of New York state's public college system, but increasingly catering to "skill set" education — nursing, early childhood education, etc. — rather than the university curricula it had been founded to provide and which carried it through most of the 1970s.

There is both good and bad in that tale. The GIs got the benefit of a university education at Harpur College. That is, they were taught how to think in the setting of the world's cultures and history. The early Baby Boomers got much the same education but, because of sheer numbers, were not welcomed into industry hungry for intelligent talent, as their fathers had been.

By the time the Baby Boom's children had arrived on campus, no pretense of *bona fide* education was attempted, and the so-called 'students' were funnelled into career tracks, generally lacking a grounding in their own culture and history, philosophy and arts and therefore able to operate the modern world, but not to understand nor influence it for the common good. In short, their education had degraded to the point of making them into pseudo-educated cogs not too intellectual to function in a dumbed-down world. That Binghamton is still ranked on an academic par with Dartmouth by some college rating services, and almost always highly ranked in "good education for the money" stats from *U.S. News & World Report* says more about the degradation of a university education across the board, perhaps, than it says about Binghamton's continuing excellence, if excellence there is.

***

Binghamton University is hardly a singular story, although it is the one with which I am most familiar, having graduated from Harpur College at the end of its heyday and just at the start of its more precipitous downward slide, some of which I witnessed. During my final year, when there were fewer applicants than in my year — the second of the Boom — the college began offering spots to ill-educated "promising" students and providing all sorts of remediation. Did it work to keep the university growing? Probably. But I also know that the tenor of discussion in classes was more pedestrian than it had been, and one had, suddenly, to take pains to lock the door to one's room and be careful not to be alone in dark places.

Granted, that is my personal experience of the slippage of a small, intense, friendly liberal arts college into a sinkhole of expansion more for the sake of grabbing state educational dollars than in remaining the crown jewel in the state's liberal arts college offerings. New York State has about 60 campuses (find a list here: http://www.suny.edu/student/campuses_complete_list.cfm).

At one time each offered a discipline that was rungs above that same discipline at the other campuses. Turning Harpur into S.U.N.Y. Binghamton was bad enough; turning it into Binghamton University — as if it had nothing to do with the powerful New York State system, one of the few with Regents exams providing at least an academic floor — was the death knell of intensive liberal education. And the beginning of the sorts of corporate problems only institutions of higher education that depend on the success of their football team for their right to exist might experience.

SUNY's mighty liberal arts college falls to athletic department greed

To say that the remedial students diluted the value of professor/student discussions would describe only one way in which this changed the nature of education at Binghamton; a look at the immense problems with criminals on its basketball team during the last decade would probably put the icing on that cake.

Following is merely one damning report on the problem:

> The report recommends hiring an 'athletic oversight officer' for the entire State University of New York system, reporting to the chancellor and Board of Trustees on admissions, the academic progress and behavior of student-athletes, and rules compliance.
>
> Citing text-message exchanges, the SUNY report also suggests Binghamton coaches made cash payments to players and assisted them with academic assignments.
>
> 'I am disappointed that a great institution like Binghamton University would, in any way, because of its athletic program, compromise its terrific academic reputation, ' SUNY chancellor Nancy Zimpher said Thursday in a conference call with reporters. (Barr, Report urges....)

The genesis of this problem was NOT the Baby Boom. It was not even Gen X, Y or Jones. It was the Greediest.

Explanation? Easy. After building extensive campuses to educate their bumper crop of kids at (in so many cases) the kids' own expense, there were campuses with extra facilities as the Baby Boom morphed into the baby bust. What to do?

Sports. Lure students and contributions with big name sports. A college like Harpur as it was first constituted had no need of, and no desire for, sports that would interfere with the academic pursuits for which students avidly attended. Students who could have gone to Dartmouth or one of the Seven Sisters had they the funding.

Once the student population had been expanded to include great numbers of job-seeker students and remedial students, however, funds would be needed to support the teaching of both, and to hold their interest, as well as encourage more such students to seek admission. Voila! And thus is born the program that allowed athletics to operate virtually devoid of contact with academics, to quite literally pay for substandard students/talented players, and to virtually give away the intellectual farm in return for a national ranking in an intercollegiate sport.

Unfortunately, it was almost undoubtedly Boomers who carried forward the programs begun when they were students leading to the Binghamton sports disaster, and so many others like it nationwide. But what were they to do? In all likelihood, it had taken them years and lots of scrambling to get a job, any job, in academia. Since they didn't have skill sets (to use a demeaning term for a person's knowledge and intelligence) that would allow them to operate in industry, and they probably had a reason or two to earn a paycheck....

That's an excuse, of course, but not a good one. They are still culpable. The thing to understand, though, is that they were at the tail end of a Ponzi scheme in education set up by none other than the Greediest.

To read Judge Kaye's report, all 102 cogent pages, visit this website:
http://a.espncdn.com/media/pdf/100211/binghamton_u_report.pdf

---

***

In addition to Cornell, Penn State also established remote campuses. Nationwide, a system of junior colleges, offering Associate Degrees in appropriate subjects or acting as funnels to Bachelor of Arts programs at four-year schools, began to appear. With all of this, naturally, came the need for more qualified faculty. And that, at last, opened the doors to Jewish intellectuals that had been closed in this nation until then. In addition, "After the war, both public and private universities sought the services of refugee-scholars, including recent arrivals from eastern Europe and the Soviet Union, even if their command of the English language was less than impeccable."(Altschuler and Blumin 2009, 91)

It is interesting to note that, while the Greediest provided increasingly job-training-style college curricula for their children, they had demanded for themselves the same sort of university learning experience developed in the great universities of Europe over hundreds of years. An initial belief among college presidents that returning GIs would choose practical courses over the university mainstay, liberal arts, proved erroneous. Especially at the more selective schools, GIs used the benefits to study languages and other cultures, having been exposed to both during their tours of duty.

There was a down side to this, however, one that would bite the children of the GIs, the Boomers. James Bryant Conant, president of Harvard after WWII, evaluated the interest in humanities subjects as "a heartening sign that the democratic process of social mobility is energetically at work, piercing the class barriers which, even in America, have tended to keep a college education the prerogative of the few." (Altschuler and Blumin 2009, 95)

For the GIs, the best; for Boomers…whatever, and less

The Greediest had demanded upward mobility via traditional university study; for their children and grandchildren, downward mobility provided by campus-based trade schools seemed good enough. It was especially good enough as long as those campuses could keep expanding and hiring construction companies even during the years of low birth rates, and offer donors — Boomer parents — a viciously competitive, pre-professional football team as well.

Indeed, in large part, while the idea that a college education was a right and that it caused upward mobility was inculcated in the Greediest' children, the Greediest conveniently forgot that the generation before them, FDR's generation, had been generous. FDR's generation had coddled the returning veterans, making sure they had money, housing, jobs, education and prospects, all without spending a dime of their own, or having to work three jobs to do it. The Greediest did not pay it forward to their own offspring — far from it, in fact.

By the time the first Baby Boomers got to college, the Greediest had decided that the Boomers could, first, fight in an unjust war and suffer derision if they served and managed to come home alive, and then pay for their own educations.

Those who served in the military in Vietnam did receive some GI benefits. But the war they fought was tougher by far than World War II, with grunts spending six times as many days per tour in combat as their fathers had, and they got less as a reward — far less — than WWII vets had done.

Nationally indefensible: National Defense Student Loans

The rest of college-age America (women and men not physically fit for the draft or unable to garner a deferment) had to pay for itself, by and large, via the National Defense Student loans. These loans were based partly on financial need, but offered various ways to reduce the principle owed, usually through teaching, and usually only those subjects approved by the government for its attention; at the time, the US government was interested in science, having lost the space race to the Russians. It must be said again: This was a far, far different educational landscape than the one the World War II GIs found themselves enjoying.

Perhaps another disheartening note for Boomers is that the generation now terrified of "socialism" in the form of universal health care and any other program except the most socialist of all, Social Security, didn't seem to mind much when the government declared that all WWII vets were equal for purposes of GI Bill educational benefits. The Bill offered the same benefit to all veterans, whether they were generals or grunts. Moreover, receiving the benefits required applicants to file "the simplest government form I have ever seen," according to Bristow Adams, an emeritus professor at Cornell. (Altschuler and Blumin 2009, 99) Aside from the simple form aspect, there could be nothing more socialist than the GI Bill, except Social Security. Neither had a means test; both were available to all comers in the identified cohort, i.e., veterans or old people.

Indeed, GI benefits were so generous and so readily available that many GIs concluded, "Why go to Podunk U. when you can go to Yale?" (Altschuler and Blumin 2009, 99) Fifty-two percent of college-bound GIs enrolled at pricey and usually excellent private colleges at public expense. "By contrast, 80 percent of veterans of the conflicts in Korea and Vietnam used their more meager tuition stipend at public colleges and universities." (Altschuler and Blumin 2009, 108) Could this be because they were not given a great apartment and spending money as well, as the WWII GIs had received? Again, no reply needed.

It is apparent that Boomers did not gain the same benefit as those who were part of the initial GI Bill cohort, the Greediest. For the Greediest, the bill boosted occupational status for the entire generation. WWII GIs who went to college on the GI Bill "enjoyed more frequent and greater laps of social mobility." (Altschuler and Blumin 2009, 107) They also had "higher incomes, more job security, better health and pension benefits, and enhanced status," (Altschuler and Blumin 2009, 107) all provided for them by the FDR generation, and denied by them to their own offspring, the Baby Boom.

Despite all that lovely free education and the upward mobility it afforded those who took advantage of the GI Bill, when Russia launched Sputnik on October 4, 1957, two things were clear. First, it was clear that the Soviet Union — the rattletrap, almost destitute Red Menace — had beaten the mighty U.S. in the space race. Indeed, that was the primary lesson America took from that occurrence.

What they missed in all of it was this: In its selfish grab for the good life and its predilection for liberal arts education, the supposedly tough fighting men of WWII had let us down.

With a dozen years to work on it, the post-War U.S. scientific community, a community that might have been more robust had the GIs chosen science instead of the classics and jobs in industry, had failed. They had returned from their limited exposure to war with an insatiable appetite for exposure to money, cars, suburban houses, and too many kids to properly educate without government assistance in the form of rising property taxes to pay for schools, for one thing. The Greediest's parents also paid those property taxes, limiting the burden on the Greediest.

Selfish seniors trash their own grandchildren's educations

When it came time for the Boomers' kids to need new schools, expanded facilities and the like, the Greediest engaged in tax revolts and refused to pay property tax increases, enacting for themselves along the way a number of local exemptions for those over 55 or so. Why? Because, the Greediest said, they didn't have any kids in school, so why should they pay taxes? Despite their "classical" educations, the simple facts of life in a republic seemed to escape them. They were so selfish, they couldn't see their way clear to help their own children provide for their grandchildren, the precise opposite of what the Greediest' parents had done for them.

What, then, was the Greeder response to the celestial superiority of their nemesis, the Soviet Union — the same nation that had decimated the German Army on the eastern front[3] so the Americans wouldn't have to?

The response was not a sort of peacetime GI Bill so that young people then coming of age and about to come of age could go to college virtually for free and have the good life, too, and maybe help us catch up in space and elsewhere. Not at all. Instead, the Baby Boom (and a small number of pre-Boomers, the Silent Generation) got the National Defense Education Act (NDEA), the means by which they would be funneled into the worklife areas Congress (then being increasingly populated by The Greediest and less by the FDR generation) mandated. To be sure, science and math were included, but it was also heavily weighted toward job training and included technical education, English as a second language (after all, someone had to get the children of the recent spate of immigrants up to speed and into the workforce), librarianship, counseling and guidance and education media center studies.

---

[3] The Siege of Leningrad was so prolonged that the Vavilov Institute, responsible for care-taking exemplars of most of the world's foodstuffs, was in danger of destruction. A handful of scientists and workers struggled to keep the seed bank intact, and particularly, the potato seeds. When, finally, they had to decide to either eat the seed potatoes (and corn and other grains), or die, they chose death. No American was faced with such a situation. If anyone wants to claim "Greatest" status, it should be the heroes of the Vavilov Institute. Without them, far more than without Norman Borlaug (called the father of the green movement because of his early genetic modifications of seeds, but actually enabler of food conglomerates and rampant third world famine as family farms disappear), world famine would be, still, far more likely. Read more about the Vavilov Institute here: http://www.ecobooks.com/authors/vavilov.htm

Note that the "...NDEA provided institutions of higher education with 90% of capital funds for low-interest loans to students. NDEA also gives federal support for improvement and change in elementary and secondary education. The act contains statutory prohibitions of federal direction, supervision, or control over the curriculum, program of instruction, administration, or personnel of any educational institution."(Columbia Encyclopedia online)

Boomers pay their own education bills, if they can get a job

These are all fine requirements. But there was a critical difference between this and the free education provided by the GI Bill. The Boomers would have to pay it back.

Moreover, the National Defense Student Loan program did not offer the loans
to students directly; rather, the government shipped the money directly to the institutions of higher learning. In addition, the loans were not granted to the parents, but rather to the students themselves. Unfortunately, there were so many Boomers that, when they graduated, there were insufficient jobs for them, and little way to pay back the loans for many of them.

This, too, opens up another avenue for social change inimical to the Boomers but neutral, at worst, for the Greediest. If they had to pay back loans, the Boomers would have to delay getting married and starting families. Possibly, with loan payback and loss of income/earning years, they would not have the time or money to have children at the same rate as the Greediest had.

The Boomers would, as it turned out, barely produce enough offspring to replace themselves, never mind contributing to population expansion. While much of this seemed acceptable to the Boomers who, after all, had suffered the indignities of overcrowding and didn't want to pass it along to their kids, it also meant fewer workers to pay for the Boomers when they got old.

Uh oh.

Out spending their childrens' inheritance…and then some

Did the Greediest plan this? Probably not. They are probably not actively culpable. But certainly, they are at least passively to blame. Or maybe actively after all. The Greediest, when they retired, moved in droves to places like Sun City, AZ, where they would not have to pay school taxes as they would living in multi-generational towns as their own fathers had done. If one simply doesn't see what's happening, there is no culpability, right? Or does a citizen have a duty to observe and participate? Whatever the correct answer to that, if one sees and ignores it, or even, as the Greediest have done, gloats over it,[4] then there is culpability. The first Greeder who bought the vanity tag sported all over Florida, "Out Spending My Children's Inheritance," issued an unmistakable manifesto, one to which the Greediest everywhere adhere. They've got theirs and they really don't give a tinker's damn whether their own children are beggared into the bargain.

---

[4] Drive around Florida, and notice how many vanity tags say "Out spending my children's inheritance." While anyone is at liberty to use their money as they see fit, there is something particularly unsettling about taking pride in trumpeting one's selfishness for all the world to see. Indeed, the Greediest seem to take delight in finding ways to say they are not doing anything for anyone.

GI Bill: Good for the Greediest. For Boomers, not so much...

The GI Bill was created as a reward for those who served in WWII, and also to prevent riots as had happened when WWI GIs returned to suffer massive unemployment. By the Vietnam era, the GI Bill had become an inducement to enlist. But even so, the program was not free to the recipients. The enlistees were required to contribute with the VA matching enlistee contributions at a rate of 2 to 1. Enlistees could contribute up to $100 each month to a maximum of $2700; they could claim these benefits — although they had contributed substantially — for only 36 months. This is radically different from the free ride the WWII GI's were granted.

Moreover, although service had to equal more than 180 days and the enlistee needed an "other than dishonorable discharge" (meaning if he or she were dishonorably discharged, he or she would lose his or her contribution) to benefit. All that began in 1973, catching a good many of the late Boomers in its net. The situation became even less attractive after July 1, 1985, when forfeiting $100 of the first year's pay was needed to result in a tuition allowance and a monthly stipend for up to 36 months of education. Approved education, or, in other words, what the Greediest in charge decided Vietnam vets were worthy of studying.

As a reward for their service in WWII, GIs were given the farm. In expectation that the next generation would save us from depredation by the dreaded communists (and despite the fact that we were off fighting communists in Asian jungles), the Baby Boom generation was told what to study and also encouraged to pay for their own education, whether civilians or military veterans.

Although the watered-down GI Bill did provide some funding to Vietnam-era veterans directly, the generous separation pay their fathers got was not provided. Many Vietnam vets trying to go to college could find only very low-paying jobs, and so had to stack up commercial loans despite serving their country and having been promised an education.

A brain is a terrible thing to waste

When those Boomers finally earned their degrees, there were still no jobs, partly because of immigration and partly because there were simply too many educated people for the jobs that required education. Often, repaying the college loans was impossible. Without help from Mom and Dad, who were busy either enjoying the good life or bearing and raising additional children, many of those students declared bankruptcy.

Great start to a successful and fulfilling life? Hardly. The financial facts of post-service life must have been especially poignant for those who had suffered through Vietnam. But the rest of the generation suffered as well. Ideologically and psychologically ripped apart by a war unnecessary on its face and unwelcome to most of the global community, but extraordinarily lucrative to the military-industrial complex run by the Greediest, the Baby Boom still experiences the PTSD of the insane dichotomy they lived through, courtesy of the older generation.

The financial distress of the Boomers was, of course, just fine with the Greediest. So fine, in fact, that they classified student loans as non-dischargeable in 1978. No other class of debt except taxes was non-dischargeable at that time. (This is a fact that would be rectified by George W. Bush, the president most emblematic of how truly bad the worst of a generation can be. George made virtually all debt non-dischargeable, putting Americans in great numbers into servitude to his cronies' financial institutions. It is shaming in the extreme to have to claim him as a member of the Baby Boom generation.)

According to the website FinAid.org:

> The US Bankruptcy Code at 11 USC 523(a)(8) provides an exception to bankruptcy discharge for education loans....
>
> Student loans were dischargeable in bankruptcy prior to 1976. With the introduction of the US Bankruptcy Code (11 USC 101 et seq) in 1978, the ability to discharge education loans was limited. Subsequent changes in the law have further narrowed the dischargeability of education debt. (Fin Aid Page LLC)

This change had the effect of making the bulk of the Baby Boom into indentured servants for college loans they had no choice but to take if they wanted to attend college. One might think the well-off parents of the Boom might have shouldered more of the cost, but one would be wrong.

Eating their young

In fact, most Boomers at public colleges combined summer work and part-time jobs, scholarships and loans to come up with the price of tuition. For much of the Boomer college years, public college tuition was about $2,000 a year. Now, it is at least five times that, and Boomers' children are not able to cobble together what their parents did, nor are they getting benefits — even as Iraq and Afghanistan combat veterans — equal to those their grandparents received under the GI Bill, nor even equal to the watered-down version the Boomer vets got.

The dilution of veterans' benefits for the Boomers was execrable; the dilution and delay of benefits for veterans of Bush's illicit wars is inexcusable. It is inexcusable philosophically and ethically, perhaps even more greatly than it is inexcusable because of the burden it places on Boomers and their children and grandchildren. The dilution of veterans' benefits, on the heels of the two Bush wars, especially, is adding insult to injury.

Even as the age 50-plus Boomers are getting laid off in droves, they are finding they must somehow pay toward their children's tuition…at the same time as 25% of the Boomers are caring for their ageing parents, either physically or financially or both. But what the heck? The 'Boomerang' children are returning to the parental nests when they are maxed out on their credit cards, anyway. According to *Aging Well* magazine:

> Parents are becoming increasingly responsible for their adult children's financial choices. Two thirds of Boomers in the Pew Research Center study believed parents should be responsible for their children's college education, as does the government. For example, emancipated students up to the age of 24 applying for federal student aid for college must report parents' income. Unfortunately, the cost of a college education has outpaced inflation, pushing parental retirement savings down the priority ladder. (Wassel 2008)

The Boomers, caring for both aged Greeder parents and "Boomerang" children who spent themselves into a stupor, are often called the Sandwich Generation, squeezed for all they are worth, and, like the filling in any tasty sandwich, eaten first.

Somehow, all of this makes the Harry Chapin song, "Cat's in the Cradle", an even better indictment of the ethos of the Greediest; of course, Chapin's ending — in which the child has become the absent father — will need to be changed to account for the fact that Boomers are not, in fact, ignoring the needs of their selfish parents. Perhaps it is time to shift the term Greatest to the Boomer generation, a move that would probably be greeted with more howling from the Greediest than any other action except, perhaps, suggesting that they don't deserve a COLA in any year when the entire economy has taken a 20 percent beating.

***

Having taken care of ourselves since the age of 18, and having been the first generation that didn't abuse our own children with cautionary tales about walking 10 miles each way to the little red schoolhouse, we are apparently going to be chewed up and spit out by both the generation before us and the one after until we drop.

And we will drop. We Boomers paid for our own educations and still started careers a few rungs behind because of the sheer numbers of us. We are now paying for our parents and for our children, without the safety net (financial and emotional) of an extended family structure (broken up by the "organization man" who transferred for dollars and spent them all on four-bedroom houses in Levittowns, et al). We are ponying up college tuitions when we should be thinking about taking care of ourselves in retirement because the defined benefit company pension disappeared right after the Greediest got theirs — if, indeed, we have not been laid off so that we can end our careers as impecuniously as we began them.

No light at the end of this tunnel

The Greediest got their educations, and allowed their own Vietnam veteran children to struggle (if they were middle or working class) as no WWII vet had to do. Boomers scrambled for scholarships, competed for scarce grants, and finally took loans they hoped to pay back when they graduated and got good jobs. Only there were not enough good jobs. There were too many Boomers, despite the best efforts of the Greediest to thin the ranks via Vietnam. Eventually, many young Boomers ended up going bankrupt, not a good start to a career and to adult life.

The Greediest' politicians had successfully shifted the burden of college costs to the students, rather than the parents, precisely in time for the Boomers to enter college. A few years later, as Boomers began to have school-age children, the Greediest repeatedly voted down bond issues to pay for new schools, leaving the children of the Boomers in the same educational abyss as the Boomers, sort of. For the Boomers, the Greediest had engineered overcrowding and fierce competition. For the children of the Boomers, the Greediest engineered substandard physical plants and "excessed" teachers, while they either scarpered off to Sun City where there were no school taxes, or moved in with their children. All of that was fairly selfish on the face of it.

But then they did the worst thing of all for American education: They (along with a number of wrong-headed and personally liable Boomers) elected George W. Bush.

Bush is nominally a Boomer. Inside, however, beats the unrepentant heart of a grasping Greeder. Like them, Bush did not have to pay for his education. Like many of them, Bush was not actually smart enough to sustain the education he was given, and like them, was pushed up the ladder of life, or, in terms prevalent in the 1980s, became an example of the Peter Principle in action.

The Peter Principle was discovered by Dr. Laurence J. Peter and Raymond Hull in their research resulting in the 1969 book, *The Peter Principle*. Peter and Hull had found that in any hierarchy (that is, a workplace), employees tend to rise to their level of incompetence.[5]

When the right-wing Heritage Foundation ginned out the idea for No Child Left Behind (NCLB), Bush adopted it as his own.

> "When school children start paying union dues, that's when I'll start representing the interests of school children." — Albert Shanker

---

[5] Because the book was published when the oldest of the Boomers who did not go to college had been in the workforce only a few years, and college-educated Boomers were just beginning to graduate, necessarily their sample had been the Greediest. How, one wonders, did Brokaw manage to miss this? To miss the fact that there was a time bomb within American industry, a glut at the top of incompetent managers who would not only prevent new and arguably more competent (or at least more energetic) workers to run things, but would put the skids under industry itself? How did he miss it? Because he had stars in his eyes, the stars of a best-seller that would appeal to the Greediest.

Shanker was born in 1928, putting him at the cusp of the Greeder/Silent Generation. He was president of the United Federation of teachers. He was also a member of the American Socialist League, which should have made him anathema to the Greediest. And yet, it is reasonable to believe that this outspoken unionist was partially responsible for transforming the profession of teaching into the job of educator. And that transmogrification of an age-old, respectable pursuit into a "skill set" probably had much to do with the initial acceptance of No Child Left Behind.

NCLB is one of the most destructive pieces of educational legislation ever conceived. It is so bad, according to CommonDreams.org, that it is, "No wonder 129 education and civil rights organizations have endorsed a letter to Congress deploring the law's overemphasis on standardized testing and punitive sanctions. No wonder 30,000 people (so far) have signed a petition at educatorroundtable.org calling the law "too destructive to salvage."(Kohn 2007)

Further:

> NCLB condemns disadvantaged students to endless rounds of testing, and no appreciable teaching for knowledge or understanding. It is "teaching to test" gone mad. Moreover, "This law cannot be fixed by sanding its rough edges. It must be replaced with a policy that honors local autonomy, employs better assessments, addresses the root causes of inequity and supports a rich curriculum. The question isn't how to save NCLB; it's how to save our schools — and kids — from NCLB. (Kohn 2007)

Saving our kids — now some Boomers' grandchildren, as well — from NCLB is the only task we have left, but it's an important one. I have no doubt most Boomers will want to carry out the task. The only question is: How many of us have been co-opted by the religious right to think of education as a bad thing? And can those who know salvation lies in education overcome the all-but-terminal dumbing down of America and pay   for   *bona   fide*   education   once   again?

CHAPTER THREE:
HOUSING, LINCHPIN OF DISASTER FOR BOOMERS

When Baby Boomers began buying houses, there were not enough to go around because the generation we followed, the Silent Generation, had been so small that not many extra houses had been needed — virtually none at all — when they became adults. There were Levittowns, of course, that had been built for the Greediest so they could create the Baby Boom, but the Greediest hadn't moved out yet. Since there were so few excess houses compared to the sudden need as Boomers came of age, prices were high.

Now that Baby Boomers want to sell their houses, downsize and retire, there are lots and lots of houses, and prices are therefore low. This part of the equation was inevitable, and perhaps we should have known — although the Greediest drummed into Boomer heads for decades that a house was the very best way to create wealth. Nothing like manipulating the market for one's own gain, regardless of whom one hurts. But then, the man in the gray flannel suit was not long on ethics. Under the GI Bill, he may have studied them in college, but apparently was a bit light on implementation.

What wasn't inevitable was that the Greediest Generation was going to take several courses of action that would make an inevitably bad situation for Boomers into a disaster. One of these inventions was, of course, the sub-prime mortgage, which some might argue was invented by the Baby Boom. It was not. Arguably Angelo R. Mozilo, CEO of Countrywide Bank and a member of the Silent Generation, began it although he had lots and lots of help.

Perhaps the first significant change to the banking laws that helped the sub-prime disaster to grow to its monstrous proportions was the Depository Institutions Deregulation and Monetary Control Act (DIDMCA) of 1980. This law allowed states to remove interest caps on commercial loans. The second bit of the equation was the Alternative Mortgage Transaction Parity Act (AMTPA) of 1982; this allowed variable interest rates to be applied to a single loan. It also allowed balloon payments.

Up, up and away: How to make Baby Boomers wish their house could fly

Balloon payments are the closest thing to casino gambling in the ostensibly staid financial industry. Bankers, seeing a client who could not afford a particular house at his or her current income, would bet the farm, so to speak, that they could save up enough to pay off the balloon when it came due.

It is, looking at it from today's post-meltdown perspective, in which criminals of the Bernie Madoff ilk have popped up repeatedly if not as massively, inconceivable that the balloon bankers thought borrowers could save up enough, or get promoted high enough and fast enough, to pay off balloon. One must conclude that perfidy was part of the equation.

At the very least, it would help to remember that it wasn't the bank's farm being wagered; it was a family's home. If the borrower's income did not rise in time to permit him or her to pay off the balloon payment, the bank could simply repossess the house. Either way, it's Bank 1, Borrower 0. Either the bank got paid, or it got a house to resell. The tales of borrowers who didn't understand what they were getting into are legion. Is it the responsibility of banks to tell them? Arguably, yes, unless those banks were the institutional version of a loan shark.

These two acts, the DIDMCA and AMTPA, set the stage for sub-prime mortgages, as well as for the financial enslavement of American consumers, when those acts were joined on the books by the Tax Reform Act of 1986. This scurrilous invention of Ronald Reagan's administration disallowed tax deductions for consumer credit interest...except for interest on mortgages. All of a sudden, it was advantageous for consumers who owned homes to transfer their credit card debt to second mortgages — quaintly named home equity lines of credit (HEL, for short) — offered by accommodating bankers.

Between them, the three acts — DIDMCA, AMTPA and the Tax Reform Act of 1986 — provided so much food for The Great White Shark Bank of the US that it is hard to imagine there was more misery in store for the consumer when they would have to swim in financial seas roiling from the Reaganite feeding frenzy. But there was, in fact, more. There was the devaluation of what little the consumer had left. There was the credit score issue to contend with.

Granting credit, taking away creditworthiness, all in one swoop

Because of the sudden entrance into the mortgage market of balloon payments — as noted, a boon to banking in every way — and the adjustable rate mortgage, another way to take a bet on a consumer's future income and, at the same time, the performance of financial markets — credit scores began to drop. Why not? If a consumer could buy a half-million-dollar home for a monthly payment of, say, $2000, with a $480,000 balloon due at the end of ten years, many people would qualify. But they would appear on paper to be, *and actually would be,* overextended.

The banks would not necessarily want to hold onto such iffy mortgages, though, and often sold them onward, piggybacking another financial market onto an already dubious primary market. Another word for the structure that evolved is, of course, pyramid scheme, one completely legalized by the gradual destruction of even minimal financial controls by government, beginning at the end of President Carter's term, and brought to fruition — at least the first round — during Ronald Reagan's faux-populist administration.

Worse was yet to come, but it would have to wait for George W. Bush. That's the bad news for the Greediest. The good news? When it came, it would punish the Boomers worst of all; this is an activity that has apparently been a prime concern of the Greediest generation since they happily identified with arch-bonehead Archie Bunker.

For the sub-prime mortgage debacle, there had to be houses

Still, the sub-prime mortgage is hardly the only factor, and it is a late one. The whole mess began with developing the suburbs out of what used to be farmland. The Greediest had help with this, in the form of loans from the United States Department of Agriculture.

In 1949, coinciding nicely with the Greediest' search for greener pastures in which to raise their intended flocks of children, the USDA developed some dandy loans "to spur home sales and development in rural areas." (Der Hovanesian 2010) While the program never was a well-known one, it nonetheless managed to pioneer some areas of loansmanship that have gotten the world into trouble recently: the $0 down, 100% financing loan. Some have described the loans as USDA sub-prime.

Without the help of the USDA and an enormous array of low- or no-downpayment mortgages and the appeal of William Levitt's Levittowns, it would have been more difficult for the Greediest to bear and raise as many children as they did. More than two children in a city apartment would be tough; more than two in a tiny tract house, however, is much, much easier. Just pack them into two tiny dormer bedrooms, and send them outside to play. While familial interaction (socialization, family values, education) diminishes, independence flourishes. In some respects, and not least due to the wide open spaces the GI Bill opened up to our fathers, we Boomers were the first generation to raise ourselves. That, too, is a good thing for the Greediest: When they want to claim the scientific advances made by Boomers, they claim it's because of them. When they want to point out that we are a strangely independent (or even squirrelly) bunch, they disavow us and claim they have no idea how we got that way. The situation is a win-win for the Greediest; it's merely a Pyrhhic victory for us Boomers to know what's happened.

The linchpin to the Boomer housing bust

While birth numbers and government-backed home loans were significant in creating the disastrous downturn in housing value just as the Boomers were ready to sell up and retire, there is another factor (besides the sub-prime debacle) that went into engineering the final takings of Boomer housing value: immigration law.

US immigration law was tinkered with by Greediest Congresses for decades in order to enhance their own enjoyment of the economy, and diminish the economy — from housing to jobs to health care to education — for the Boomers. (It must be mentioned that managing immigration also had a desirable effect on Greediest employment, and a disastrous one on Boomer employment.

Housing, housing everywhere

"Asset prices may well decline as the large number of future retirees sell the homes and equities they accumulated in anticipation of retirement."
(Clark et al 2004, 80)

This quote is fine as far as it goes. Indeed, if any Baby Boomer who was over-invested in personal real estate had thought about it, *of course* their own retirement and a move to smaller lodgings would return homes to the market, causing something of a glut and bringing prices down. That would effectively diminish their retirement nest egg to a degree, a large degree compared to the house-hungry Boom market into which the Greediest Generation sold its homes at retirement age. They sold them to us, to the Baby Boomers, at wildly inflated prices both because of the dearth of available housing, and because of the raging inflation in the 1970s, when so many Boomers were beginning their working/family lives.

But imagine that, for Boomers, the compression factors of housing resale is compounded by two additional factors: The Baby Boom had far fewer children than needed even to replace themselves, thus creating excess housing even before they would need to sell out to downsize and retire, and the Greediest Generation was so phobic about illegal aliens that they had put the brakes on immigration so effectively that, at least in the U.S., immigration did not do much, if anything, to drive up the value of housing.

That is not true in western Europe, where, because of the European Union, immigration from the poorer former eastern bloc nations is driving housing values up, in general, in the NATO nations. Because of the EEC, precursor to the EU, some amount of this has been a factor since 1957, when the EEC was founded to create a common market among Belgium, France, Germany, Italy, Luxembourg and the Netherlands. By the 1980s, the consortium also included Denmark, West Germany, Portugal, Greece, Spain, Ireland and the United Kingdom.

In 1993, the European Union was formed out of the EEC, including 27 member states to begin with, but capable of expansion. It counts within current member states almost 500 million citizens; the EU combined generates 30% of gross world product. To do that, citizens of member nations move across national borders at will to take jobs and buy housing where the economy is booming. The capability to shift large numbers of people is vexing to many Europeans who miss the cultural cohesiveness of pre-EU Europe. But it does seemingly allow for a more stable and sensible approach to the expansion and contraction of markets than does the monolithic, generally isolationist immigration stance of the United States.

Like almost every political action since 1945, retaining a ferocious independence, even from close neighbors like Canada and Mexico, has benefitted the Greediest and put the Boomers at risk. The Greediest have used immigration for a very effective two-pronged attack on the Baby Boom, via both housing and jobs.

In fact, the effect on jobs was probably more immediate, having its effects felt from the moment the first 18-year-old Boomer took a job at $1.25 an hour (minimum wage in 1964, a figure now estimated to equal about $7.14 adjusted for inflation[6]) until the recent spate of layoffs, which followed a decade or more of downsizings in which the oldest, most expensive workers read the pink slips first. However, in early 2010 — with the financial crisis/recession still very much with us — it is the issue of housing that will get the first exposure.

***

Tales from the "houses are the best investment" crypt

In the late 1970s, Ted and Alice bought a Mizner house in Delray Beach, FL. Mizner houses were the cream of the crop for old Florida homes. In the 1920s, an untrained architect named Addison Mizner had moved to Palm Beach and almost single-handedly caused the Florida renaissance by designing nouveau Spanish-style homes for the nouveau riche who were seeking the sun closer to home than Cannes.

---

[6] In July, 2009, the US federal minimum wage was $7.25. Boomers, if they were entering the job market now, would do at least marginally better than they did in 1964. But then, the Boomers are more generous to their offspring than the Greediest. The problem is, of course, that because of the Reagan-Bush combination of ludicrous economics, unbridled greed and stupefying ignorance, few Boomer children have jobs, and Boomers themselves, stripped of all they worked for in the debacle, are competing with their own children and grandchildren for low-wage jobs.

It was a bit of a stretch for their budget at the time; Ted and Alice had two young children to raise. But they decided to do it because, they thought, the house could not help appreciating and would provide a good chunk of their retirement nest egg when they sold it. Dave, a law enforcement officer, could retire relatively early and they wanted to enjoy life for a while, like anyone else.

When Ted and Alice were barely 40, they decided to sell the Mizner house and invest the money. Their eldest child was grown and gone, and it didn't make sense to live in such big house when they could sell, invest the profits, buy a smaller house, pay it off or nearly so in 15 years of part-time work, and still retire nicely.

About the time they decided to sell, in 1987, a neighbor who knew about this asked them to delay selling their house because he was older and wanted to sell his and, he claimed, it would hurt both their sales prices if there were two For Sale signs on the block.

They agreed. And then the neighbor, who owned a large corner Mizner house, sold his house as a group home for anorexic women in recovery...or so he said. That would have been bad enough in a quiet, residential neighbhorhood from which one could walk to the beach, if one were sufficiently motivated. In fact, he sold it to a slumlord who filled it full of illegal immigrants who kept chickens in the yard, dried laundry on the hedges, and smoked ganga on the terrace. Overnight, the value of Ted and Alice's house declined so much that they very nearly *lost* money — cold, hard cash — selling it. They did lose 60 percent of the nest egg they had planned, and scraped, to build.

Their neighbors across the street, who had bought just a year earlier but had a compelling business reason to move back north right about that time, lost more than $35,000 on their house, their entire downpayment. Needless to say, that house had not appreciated, either, after the corner house sold.

The neighborhood became a slum over the next couple of years. The seller of the corner house had his money out and had moved happily into a retirement haven. The seller of the corner house, as well as the slumlord, were both members of the Greediest Generation. So was the man to whom Ted and Alice's neighbors sold their house. Indeed, he was the father of the person they had bought the house from. He was a Greeder. There is little doubt that he convinced his own daughter and son-in-law to sell the house to the couple from the north. The son-in-law didn't want to sell, really — it had been his childhood home, and he had lavished care on it.

The man had to sell so that his Greeder father-in-law and his zoning board cronies trashed the neighborhood, it wouldn't be his own children he was raping, but someone else's. That's just life as usual in the jungle world the Greediest inhabit. One might easily ask, is it any wonder Boomers have always taken social causes to heart? Deep down inside, they knew their parents' generation was reptilian, and would eat everyone's children but their own. And maybe their own as well.

***

The experience of Ted and Alice and the entire neighborhood should have constituted a dire warning to any Baby Boomer living in the area at the time. Ted and Alice's neighbors, the ones who lost $35,000, had known the Greediest Generation would eat their lunch sooner or later, but they thought they had at least 15 or 20 years to watch their home appreciate when they bought it.

In 1983, one of them had written *The Complete Social Security Handbook,* published by Dodd, Mead. While researching it, they realized that it was highly unlikely Social Security would do for them, or for any Baby Boomer, what it was doing for their parents. Indeed, they were so concerned about the future of Social Security—and thus the old age of the largest generation in the history of the world in the wealthiest nation in the world—that they wrote a book called *Eating Their Young: The Birth and Rape of the Baby Boom.* Their agent had peddled it all over New York and not a single publishing house would touch it, despite the reliable, accurate journeyman reputation in the book trade of its two authors. Their own agent suggested taking the manuscript to an agent with a reputation for being able to sell any manuscript about anything.

He failed, too. He mentioned that the reason might be that the very people engineering the eating of the Baby Boom were in charge of the publishing houses.[7]

---

[7] This is not that book, although one of the same authors has written this one. Then, the only notable avenue of inquiry seemed to be Social Security. Since then, especially in the aftermath of the Bush financial meltdown, it became clear that a constellation of political/government maneuverings were essential contributors to the disaster facing today's aging Baby Boomers...and so new research, with attention to current realities, was undertaken.

Revealing Social Security as wealth transfer

Two things were abundantly clear. The fix was in with Social Security. When the Social Security book was written, most people thought Social Security was insurance, and that the "insurance" company was investing the premiums and that was providing the payments in retirement.

Many people still think that.

But they're wrong. They have always been wrong. Social Security has always transferred money from those currently working and paying FICA taxes to those currently retired and receiving benefits. Another word for it is wealth transfer. Note: Recipients get "benefits," not distributions. What they get is a 'beneficence' not a natural result of investment.

Cunningly, the Greediest Generation was in charge of Congress, too, and so was able to increase the beneficence to its own generation dramatically; after all, the next generation, the Baby Boom, would be paying for it. And lord knows, there were lots of them. The fact that their incomes had not increased in real terms, as had those of the Greediest during their early working years, also escaped notice by the Greediest Generation.

How to overcome the Social Security deficit, or not

Knowing about that fix, especially after the reinforcement of having every viable New York publisher return the manuscript to an incredibly powerful agent, the authors moved south. They figured that, in years to come, if worse came to worst, they could at least eat the mangoes growing on huge trees in the yard of the house they bought, and go fishing. They were preparing for their retirement the best way they knew how, by using the common wisdom: They bought a house. It's your greatest asset, common wisdom had assured them, and at the very least, they figured they'd have a paid-off place to live in when they reached retirement age, if they didn't sell it sooner and invest the proceeds.

But after Black Monday (the stock market crash of October 19, 1987), they had to sell early; their major client had gone belly up in the Black Monday debacle, and they needed to be back in NYC to rebuild their business. That major client, who ran a boutique executive report publishing house, was heavily invested in the stock market, and also more leveraged than he had wanted to be after buying his office building and more printing equipment at exactly the wrong moment.

As plainly writ as was the greediness of the Greediest Generation to the two authors after their Social Security research, they still believed the fiction that housing would appreciate regardless of what else happened in an economy over the long term. That common wisdom, developed by the Greediest, is that appreciation would accrue irrespective of improvements made, when the area it's in becomes more desirable, or when there are more buyers looking for houses than there are houses to buy. It was possible—even probable, they thought—that Delray Beach would become more desirable.

The rot in the middle of Florida's "New England" town

Delray Beach is a quaint, New England-style town on the Atlantic Ocean halfway between Fort Lauderdale and Palm Beach. What could go wrong? *Of course*, it would become even more desirable. There was a new outdoor Spanish-style shopping galleria going in just across the Intracoastal Waterway from a great beach club. People were moving to Florida in droves, still. The economy was booming, with a bull market that had begun shortly after Ronald Reagan became president.

Everyone figured the "trickle down" theory would cover them with at least a bit of the financial milk and honey; what they hadn't figured on was that Reagan had packaged the "secret sauce" in a bottle with no holes as far down as most Americans were standing. Only those who could already lick the top of the bottle were likely to gain any sustenance. And, with their long sticky tongues — decreasing taxes, free-for-all financial environment — they could reach right in and suck off the sauce the lower folk could have gotten if only there had been any holes.

Wrong turn, back to Delray Beach

There was to be inward migration to Delray Beach all right, but it wouldn't be people who would pay top dollar for an historic Mizner house, nor for the more modest house, built in 1938 of cypress, across the street. It was to be immigrants with no money and no legal right of residency. It would be some of the most disadvantaged immigrants on the planet, Haitians. By 2000, Delray Beach ranked number 16 in percentage of Haitian immigrants in its population in the United States, outranking a dozen other cities and locales in Florida.(Haitian ancestry website)

It is also, according to the United States Tennis Association, one of the top tennis towns in the US, and has been since a top tournament moved there in 1999.

Ten years ago, I revisited that neighborhood. The immigrants were gone, and the houses had become B-2 offices for attorneys and the like.

Three years ago, I visited again. The houses had turned back into houses, but seemed to be rentals catering to lower-income residents, not culturally and economically disadvantaged islanders escaping misery, but mainly Anglos with low-paying jobs. The main street in the neighborhood was, however, where the truth was writ large.

In the 1980s, those streets had a variety of local businesses catering to middle-class residents. Dry cleaners. A Publix supermarket and a drug store. A movie rental place. A couple of hairdressers. A bank. A craft shop.

Now those streets are lined with high-rise condominiums and upscale boutiques and restaurants. In the 1980s, the area was not zoned for high-rises. But why would the zoning commission object to that sort of "improvement" after the surrounding area had become a slum? Answer: They wouldn't. There is every reason to believe that the neighborhood was trashed so that those who wanted to profit from development of high rises on the edge of an environmentally sensitive area — the Intracoastal Waterway — could get zoning changed to permit it.

Anecdotal evidence aside, what has become of the Baby Boom's biggest asset, the very one we were told over and over and over to consider the linchpin of our retirement nest eggs?

We Boomers are culpable. We forgot how few children we were having, how much overbuilding there was in desirable areas like Florida and the DC beltway…and how totally the Greediest didn't care what happened to the economy or anyone in it as long as they prospered.

Boomers' retirement nest egg was fried and eaten in a delicious Boomer sandwich

In February, 2009, the Senate Special Committee on Aging held a hearing. The following information is from the testimony of economist Dean Baker, co-director of the Center for Economic and Policy Research (CEPR). Based on the Federal Reserve Board's 2004 Survey of Consumer Finance, Baker made these projections.

> 1) The median household with a person between the ages of 45 to 54 saw their net worth fall by more than 45 percent between 2004 and 2009, from $150,500 in 2004, to just $82,200 in 2009 (all amounts are in 2009 dollars). This figure, which includes home equity, is not even sufficient to cover half of the value of the median house in the United States. *In other words, if the median late Baby Boomer household took all of the wealth they had accumulated during their lifetime, they would still owe more than half of the price of a typical house in a mortgage and have no other assets whatsoever." (Emphasis added)*

> 2) The situation for older Baby Boomers is similar. The median household with a person between the ages of 55 and 64 saw their wealth fall by almost 38 percent from $229,600 in 2004 to $142,700 in 2009. This net worth would be sufficient to allow these households, who are at the peak ages for wealth accumulation, to cover approximately 80 percent of the cost of the median home, if they had no other asset. (2009)

You've heard the term upside down regarding mortgages? That is a horrific enough thought if you are young, still have some peak earning years ahead of you, and bought either in a boom market or with a sub-prime loan.

What if you are, however, a hard-working person of about 60, your prime earning years gone, and you are among the 15 percent of older Boomers, those between ages 55 and 64, who will need to bring money to the closing when they sell their homes? Is this not about as far from financing one's golden years via one's real estate as possible? This age group will be as locked out of the market as first-time buyers, or worse. First-time buyers usually borrow from mom and dad. For the Boomers, they ARE mom and dad. For them, there is no recourse.

No recourse for older Boomers

That bears repeating: Older Boomers, who delayed childbearing because of the Vietnam war, paying off college loans and finding jobs (and even then, at flat wages) in a job market manipulated by the Greediest, and who may have spent the past ten years caring for Greeder parents, are out of funds and almost out of time.

For older Boomers, THERE IS NO RECOURSE.

In addition to the 15 percent of Baby Boomers in a negative equity position, there are hundreds of thousands more at a break-even point; while they may be able to sell their homes, after 25 or 30 years of caring for that home and paying for that home, and drinking the home-appreciation Kool-Aid served up early and often by the Greediest, they will gain nothing when they sell. Not a dime to put into a smaller home, a retirement apartment, or any amenities at all. Not a nickel to use when the Social Security payments they get have been reduced, through the understandable efforts of their own children and grandchildren not to pay half their salaries in taxes. Not a penny to use to buy prescription medicines under Mr. Bush's execrable modification of the Medicare pharmaceuticals benefit, should it not be revised by Mr. Obama's or subsequent administrations.

Like their parents and grandparents, the Boomers "planned their consumption and saving with the assumption that their house price would continue to appreciate, or at least not decline in value," Baker's testimony noted (2009). Unlike their parents and grandparents, they did not profit from that assumption.

Political causes of Boomer distress

Traditionally, political conservatives vote in favor of laws that benefit corporations, and certainly, shifting the retirement burden from government (which was paying their benefits at the time, or about to be) to the Baby Boom suited Greeder voters to a T. In a 2009 Gallup survey, people 65 and older (which includes both the Greediest and the tiny "nowhere" generation, the Silent Generation to which, for example, Tom Brokaw belongs) were the most likely of any generation to self-identify as Conservative, at 48%.

Thirty-five percent of that group self-identified as moderate, and only 16 percent as liberal.

Boomers, too, however, were more conservative than most people might think, considering their apparently liberal bias early in the generation's trip toward adulthood. There was almost no difference in self-identification between older and younger Boomers (although the younger set also incorporates the Gen Xs), with Older Boomers at 42 percent conservative, 37 percent moderate and 20 percent liberal; Younger Boomers identified at 41 percent conservative, 36 percent moderate and 21 percent liberal. The youngest cohort, voters 18 to 29 years of age, were predominately moderate, at 39 percent, with conservatives (30 percent) and liberals (31 percent) an almost even split. (Gallup 2010)

Still, the laws governing Baby Boom retirement were voted into place by a cohort that self-identifies, even in the aftermath of the Obama liberal "revolution," as conservative. How much more likely is it that this cohort, and especially the older "older" portion, has consistently approved all legislation extending power and emoluments to corporations, and withdrawing them from individuals?

Empirically, with the corporate haste to abandon their responsibility to those who make their money (their employees) in favor of stockholders (who produce nothing except the toxic paper products the US and most of the world has grown to love), it is obvious that indeed, the Greediest have stacked the deck. Their house of cards has now fallen — as they probably knew it would and didn't care — on their mainly unsuspecting offspring. The thing is, of course, the destruction of financial regulation in the nation was so complete, being given its final push by an older, Republican Congress during Clinton's first term, that the house of cards had a brick on top of it when it fell. And that brick has virtually crushed the first half of the Baby Boom generation, and has maimed the second, as well as setting up all their offspring for the "genetic" disease of economic catch-up.

Greeders to Boomers: Look out, we're about to rob you blind!

If you still doubt that the Baby Boom was simply raw meat to the Greediest Generation, note Baker's cogent conclusion. The Baby Boom, he said, "were the victims of the largest intergenerational transfer of wealth in the history of the world, as they disproportionately incurred the loss of $8 trillion in housing wealth and $7 trillion in stock wealth."(Baker 2009)

The Greediest are, on the other hand, sitting pretty. The Baby Boom's parents:

- Have already gotten most of the benefit of the Social Security and Medicare systems; Bought retirement housing when it was relatively inexpensive;
- Shifted the cost of educating their children (the Baby Boom) to those very children, and;
- Continue to vote for corporate interests and against social welfare initiatives (Gallup 2010) as if to do so would be to put hemlock to their own lips (they prefer to let their children drink the bitter cup.)

The Boomers' children and grandchildren will, in a perverse way, be the beneficiaries of this loss, since they will be able to buy the country's stock of housing and corporate capital at prices that are 30-50 percent less than what they would have faced just two years ago. (Remember, though, that it is almost inescapable that their payroll taxes to bankroll the transfer plan/pyramid scheme known as Social Security, will rise, giving them no net gain, in the end.) While there is nothing Boomers can or should do to reverse this enormous intergenerational transfer (two wrongs do not make a right), Congress can act to protect the social insurance programs on which the Baby Boomers will be dependent. Social Security and Medicare have long been the bedrock of the country's social safety net.

They will be more important than ever as the Baby Boomers enter their retirement years, robbed of an old age of relative comfort by their parents' greed...as they were robbed of their youth by their parents' romps between the sheets and cavalier attitude toward caring for the children they produced.

It would pay Boomers to remember that they were part of an enormous human litter, created by a cohort whose only aim seems to be personal aggrandizement whether in numbers of children or cars in the driveway.

It would pay them to recall being robbed of their youth by having to compete viciously for grades, for space at the table, for parental and teacher attention, for a deferment of service in an immoral war being fed on the bodies of the best educated GIs in history; 79% had a college diploma or better (McCaffrey 1993), leading to the seminal discussion of the Greediests' invention and conduct of the Vietnam war, *The Best and the Brightest* by David Halberstam.

It would pay them to recall that they were robbed of their young adulthood by their parents' stinginess in shifting educational costs to the Baby Boom, and sending them to die in an Asian jungle to stoke the war machine that kept the Greediest fully employed and racking up Social Security benefits they would be the last generation to receive in full, despite paying a fraction of what the enormous Boomer generation, many of them working at the low end of the earnings scale but relatively higher end of the FICA scale, most of their lives.

What's next for aging Boomers?

Communes, that's what's next for Boomers, or, alternatively, life on the street.

Forcing the Baby Boom into communes

In March, 2009, Alexander Zaitchick, writing on AlterNet, painted a gloomy picture of Boomer retirement housing.

He noted that, "Among the adjustments forced by the new circumstances, perhaps the cruelest twist for many Boomers is the need to join younger generations in the roommate queue."(Zaitchick 2009)

Fortunately, the Boomers virtually invented the American commune; there was not enough affordable housing when we were 18, so we doubled up. Indeed, in many colleges, dorms were "tripled," with three students housed in a two-student room. The Boomers are no strangers to crowded conditions.

Still, those Boomers who made the transition from group living to a home of their own can be little but dismayed at the current turn of events. Zaitchik reported:

> 'In the last few months we've experienced explosive growth in interest by homeowners age 50-plus to find rooms and roommates,' says Jacqueline Grossmann, Chicago coordinator for the National Shared Housing Resource Center. 'The trend now is getting younger and younger. People in their 50s and 60s are losing their nest

eggs and increasingly willing to give up their privacy in exchange for rents of $500, $600 a month.' (Zaitchick 2009)

If you doubt that this trend is evidence of a disaster in the land, Zaitchik also reported this comparison to another recent disaster, exacerbated by government incompetence or downright hostility:

> 'We've seen a 400 percent increase over the last few months of people nearing retirement age,' says Rita Zadoff, director of Housemate Match, a shared-housing program serving the Atlanta area. 'We haven't been this busy since we helped Katrina victims find housing.' (Zaitchick 2009)

Recently, when the remaining Greediest were getting truly tottery, elderly clients were mainly seeking a "protective presence" in the form of younger people sharing their home, according to Zaitchik's report. Recently, however, it is much younger people — the 50s and 60s — with too much house and too little income looking for help with mortgage or utility payments.

The many home-share organizations that are involved were founded in order to help the disabled and very elderly. That they are now helping retiring or close-to-retiring Boomers means simply that the Boomers — after a lifetime of work in a nation that has treated their own parents superbly well — are in the same boat as their own children and grandchildren (a condition historically associated with youth and short worklife-to-date): They are broke. They are flat, dead, hopelessly broke, no better off than the family-less oldsters shunted off to poor farms in the 19th century. Paupers, who were mainly the elderly without means or extended families and the disabled, were housed in common residences supported by the town or city. They were common nationwide until the Social Security Act of 1935, and most had disappeared by about 1950.

The "Wayback Machine" has been dismantled

Even if they wanted to, poor elders can no longer count on bed and board from the communities they've worked and lived in all their lives. So it's either communes, or life on the street.

***

Broke is, of course, relative. Not having the cost of tomorrow's milk is far different from seeing one's retirement nest-egg disappear, but possibly no less disheartening. Indeed, it might be more traumatic. After all, not having the price of tomorrow's milk is often the result of a very palpable disaster: war, famine, widespread epidemics and such. And, of course, as noted, it has virtually not happened here since fifteen years after the inception of Social Security...since fifteen years after the Greediest' *parents* took the steps to protect the Greeder generation in its old age from what they themselves and generations before had suffered.

A recent report by the Center for Economic and Policy Research, "The Wealth of the Baby Boom Cohorts After the Collapse of the Housing Bubble," reveals just how bad it is, just how impoverished they are and in many cases how impossible is the retirement of the Baby Boom, versus the retirement of the Greediest. (Rosnick)

Zaitchik quotes a report that "details how the collapse has left the majority of those around retirement-age almost completely reliant on entitlements. The net worth of median households in the 45 to 54 age bracket has dropped by more than 45 percent since 2004, to just over $80,000. Households headed by those aged 55 to 64, meanwhile, have lost 38 percent of net wealth. (Zaitchick 2009).

The result? One of the authors of that report is quoted as saying "many Baby Boomers will only have entitlements to rely on in their retirement." (Zaitchick 2009)

Entitlements. Meaning Social Security. A bankrupt program into which the Greediest paid little, and Boomers have poured much. Since it as a "we-pay-as-they-go" scheme, that meant we were generous with our parents, albeit because they controlled the Congress and kept voting for those who would establish more benefits for them and higher taxes for us. There is not much room to push those taxes up again, particularly as the very small generation behind the Baby Boom will be unlikely to accept a taxation rate of 50% of earnings, which is what it would take to provide for us as we provided for our parents.

Our entitlements, after the income transfer begun after World War II, ramped up by Reagan, fine-tuned by Bush I, and exported globally by Shrub to his Saudi friends and others whose lust for wealth is as infinite as the desert sands, will amount to squat.

So, because we will have little choice, squat we will...in shared housing.

***

Is what's good for the goose also good for the gander?

A platoon of commentators has opined that it is better for the aging to live in close proximity to each other, for mutual aid and so on. They contend that it is ludicrous for older people to be driving out one by one for groceries and to the eye doctor for their cataract surgery follow-ups.

Possibly. But if it is so socially, fiscally and environmentally horrific for individual retirees to live independently, why, then, have Boomers spent half of their adult lives ensuring that their own parents, the Greediest, can do exactly that? Zaitchick (2009) asked, "With the nation full of worthless, ridiculously large, and mostly empty houses, why not fill them with the newly penurious and like-minded Boomers in need of housing?"

Because, for one thing, it is infantilizing Boomers before their time. The Greediest fought long and hard to keep from being infantilized, (Zaitchick 2009) to keep from being sent to the retirement home when it was a full-time job for their children to chauffeur them to appointments, keep track of them during early Alzheimers and such. Lifestyles are born out of the society in which people live; in the United States, independence is, *a priori*, part of that lifestyle. Not to put too fine a point on it, but it is all but written into the Constitution. It is our image, our quest. It is a gift we (and their parents) gave to the Greediest; it is a gift they have done everything in their power to deny to us and to our children and to our children's children.

It is difficult to disagree with Zaitchick's notion that it would be better to build tightly knit communities or abandon the suburbs completely for urban core housing. But it was the Greediest (aided and abetted by the USDA and William Levitt et al) who invented the suburbs, mainly to house their overlarge families and overwhelming desire for the good life that had been out of reach until the generation that felt guilty for World War I and probably World War II feathered the Greediest' nests for them. But individual housing in a small, efficient community is far different from sharing living quarters with strangers in the wilds of suburbia and exurbia, where cars are de rigueur and camaraderie is limited to housemates.

Some Boomers are less dismayed at the idea of a communal end to their lives than others. Zaitchick tells the story of a psychologist whose retirement savings dropped 60 percent, putting an end to her plan of spending her retirement in Europe and New York City, living off the IRA and savings. She had lived communally in the 1970s, however. Not all Boomers — not even many, all things considered — had that experience or have the willingness to experience it now.

There are studies that show people feel less lonely, safer, and happier in shared communities, whether that's a commune, group-owned home or shared apartment. Perhaps. But the fact that this is the first generation *forced* to experiment with these lifestyle formats says it all; Zaitchick noted that even though many Boomers' kids haven't yet begun paying mortgages of their own (and if they had, perhaps Boomers' houses might sell), having Boomers live in group homes means they will call on their own children for help less often.

There can be little doubt where the term Sandwich Generation to describe Boomers came from; it came from accurate observation of the estate the Greediest have arranged for their own children, that estate being the tasty filling that holds two slices of bread together. On their own, the two slices of bread are nothing. But the Greeder slice has spent years convincing the Boomers that they were and still are "rotten kids." The Boomers' children, having been spared the overcrowding their parents experienced and having been given toys unimaginable even in the 1960s, spend most of their time bashing Boomers, pinning the recent debacles on them with no regard for history, and certainly none for their parents. Yet, without the Boomers — whom the children run home to sponge off of at will — the next generation would be a gormless slice of white bread, too, and unable to stand on its own.

***

To recap the facts:

- The Boomers bought housing at high prices because their own parents procreated with no thought to the welfare of their offspring.
- The Boomers were quite generous to their parents, and gave them everything the parents hadn't already given themselves via Social Security COLAs and Medicare.
- The Boomers, who barely made a blip in their parent's trek toward an abundant old age, will now relieve their own children of having to pay them any attention or concern by living in communes because of the financial debacle the Greediest wrought.

It is possible the young will step up to the plate to some extent; but bear in mind that by the time half of today's Baby Boom is retired, it will cost one of every two tax dollars to support them. How many young people, busy raising their own families and planning for retirement, will put up with that? They won't.

Already, they are to be found all over the Internet, uselessly and viciously bashing the Boomers, and wrongly thinking that the Boomers are singularly responsible for current realities just because Greeder Wannabe Bush was born physically into the cohort.

Bush would be, of course, deficient in any cohort, almost too deficient to be blamed. Which brings it all back to his daddy and Ronald Reagan, cowboy architect of the trickle-down cesspool all but the top 2 percent of America is trying to find a way out of.

CHAPTER FOUR:
FOOD SCIENCE, DEADLY SCIENCE

The problem with America's food is that the almost totally anti-intellectual scientists of the World War II generation ran roughshod over the nation's agricultural community with no input from philosophers (certainly a type of thinker anathema in that can-do era, and still frowned upon), sociologists or even working farmers.

The legacy for the Baby Boom is this: We were raised on canned vegetables, nutrients flushed away at the processing plant or the kitchen sink, and are now being all but forced to buy Frankenfood, genetically altered plant and animal material that's nothing at all as nature intended. Rather than having most of our food come from farms reasonably close to where we live, the expansion of the highways — the Eisenhower Interstate System — meant it was possible and profitable to ship strawberries from southern California to New York in the fall, fresh lettuce from Florida to Minnesota in January and so on. The impact on the food itself is falling levels of nutrients through storage, shipping and handling. The impact on the food industry — which is what it had become and no longer farming or even agriculture — was to employ food scientists to make ever tougher fruits and vegetables to withstand the manhandling, never mind the nutritive or taste values.

That was the first generation of research. Now, it is even more frightening than that. In 2007, author Darien Ibrahim noted, "Corporations are now doing genetic research designed to create animals with more 'efficient' traits; for example, by growing chickens with no feathers and animals with no legs."(2007, 89+) Ibrahim attributes the information to a speech by the director of the Animal Research Institute at a Livestock Intensive Methods of Production Conference in 1978, some of it later reported in Broiler Industry (January 1979, 98).

So, we have strawberries all year round that look like red ping-pong balls and taste like a combination of plasterboard and kindergarten white glue. Supermarkets offer hard peaches and pears that rot before ripening. Blueberries have skins, these days, that would do for making "pleather" wallets, and a flavor that makes potassium alum taste sweet by comparison; perhaps they should simply be called puckerberries.

Would you like some deformed muscle of lamb for dinner?

Food scientists do something to Brussels sprouts so cooks can leave them in a plastic bag and microwave them; processors pare all the goodness off of big carrots, carve them into myriad little ones, and charge an arm and a leg for "baby" vegetables with no flavor but that will last in the fridge for a month. Shortly, we might have "deformed leg muscle of lamb" because they will have no legs *per se*; at least it will eliminate the pastoral picture of fluffy lambs playing in green fields some struggle with when eating lamb.

How is all this the fault of the greediest generation?

A short history of the USDA after World War II[8] will hint at how the current conditions, with edible plant material substituting for nutritious food in adequate variety, came to be.

---

[8] Please see Housing chapter for additional ways the USDA ensured wealth for the Greediest and poverty for the Baby Boom.

Add to that the development of the Interstate Highway system, and one has the blueprint for the distributed food industry from which we currently suffer. Without the tinkering of the USDA and the construction of highways — added to the ability to refrigerate and freeze foods that had been developed earlier in the twentieth century — it would have been difficult to pick, sort, pack, store, ship and redistribute foodstuffs over great distances efficiently.

It came down to trucks, because trains, which can go only where the tracks go, were not up to the task of distributing out-of-season produce nationwide.

Nor were local distribution vectors, which were a patchwork of small companies, able to gather produce in central warehouses for redistribution in a UPS-style hub-and-spoke system. It took the evil triumvirate of the USDA, the highway system, and refrigeration/freezing to make our foodstuffs into ersatz edibles that deliver a pre-selected package of nutrients (not necessarily those nature intended) in forms with a long shelf life, and almost no palate appeal. Even without the wealth transfer involved in all of this, the spiritual impoverishment for Americans would be stunning. (And the fact that Americans do experience spiritual impoverishment regarding food is clear from the 2008 recession; one of the first publications to disappear because of lack of reader, and thus advertiser, support was *Gourmet*.)

More than one health guru has suggested we are so fat because, partly, we keep eating to try to find the satisfaction in eating that Big Ag and the food scientists have removed from food. (And which, to belabor the point, *Gourmet* had long attempted to show us how to overcome.) Others say it's the presence of

High Fructose Corn Syrup, which has been front and center among suspect foods in recent years.[9]

It is probably both, and more. Chemicals. Packaging residues. Preservatives....And just lately, a health guru named Dr. Joseph Mercola, writing for *Huffington Post*, noted that "aspartame was previously listed by the Pentagon as a biochemical warfare agent!" (2010)

The South as the poster child for USDA abuses

In his ebook, *The USDA Legacy: From the New Deal to Silent Spring*, Pete Daniel chronicles the destruction of American agrarian practice by the USDA. The ebook was published by Historical Text Archives, one of the oldest such sites on the Internet.

Daniel's main interest is the South, where the New Deal's Agricultural Adjustment Administration (Triple A) wildly expanded the federal presence on southern farms. The AAA was created in 1933, and altered agriculture so that, far from helping the tenant farmers and sharecroppers who produced so much food and cotton, it virtually destroyed them, replacing them with landlords who took and hoarded federal farm monies until they could buy tractors and then eliminate many of their tenants and sharecroppers, replacing them with hired labor who had no interest in the land or in the quality of the crops; their main interest was the paycheck, followed by the

---

[9] "The bid to rename the sweetener by the Corn Refiners Association comes as Americans' concerns about health and obesity have sent consumption of high fructose corn syrup to a 20-year low.

"The group plans to apply Tuesday to the Food and Drug Administration to get 'corn sugar' approved as an alternative name for food labels." (Fredrix, 2010).

chance to run the machinery, a job that no doubt beat digging ditches or other manual labor hands down. Thus, the landowners once again became the local elite, as they had been before the Civil War when they simply owned the workers rather than the machines that now did the work and displaced the workers.

Midwestern intellectuals, Daniel notes, wrestled with the USDA about these maneuvers, but, by the late 1930s, had lost to the increasingly powerful agribusiness interests, interests that would doubtless use the absence of young men to the armed services as an excuse to push their industrialized agriculture agenda even more forcibly. "During World War II the victors consolidated their power," Daniel (2009) notes. Apparently, the generous parents of the GIs were not monolithic; more than vestiges remained of the robber baron mentality of an earlier era.

Was blueprint factory farming the death knell of family farming?

That wasn't the only factor involved in turning family farming into agriculture into corporate agriculture. In the 1950s, idiocy held sway throughout the USDA. Overlapping programs and programs that completely ignored local climate, topography, soils, preferences and so on were the norm. Louisiana farmer Wilbert McReynolds succinctly explained to Benson in the mid-1950s that farm failures "may be the result of trying to make an Iowa plan fit Louisiana."(Daniel 2009)

Needless to say, any advice the remaining farmers got from the USDA was useless at best, and hastened the demise of farms at worst.

Racism rules in farm country

After Brown v. Board of Education in 1954, as the push for total integration and voting rights began to expand, USDA bureaucrats denied credit to black farm owners, while shoveling money toward white farmers. (Schapsmeier 1992) Aside from the unethical nature of the USDA actions and their possible illegality, the practice also served to funnel more African Americans to the cities where they would have to learn a living any way they could. There's little call for tractor running skills in downtown Chicago. In addition, uprooting families from where they had lived for generations took its toll on everyone involved.

Paid for not working; Paid even more for storing the excess

While all this was going on, improvements in farm implements and seeds were allowing farmers to produce far more than the market would bear; farmers were paid by the government *not* to produce crops. Still, there was too much food and the USDA had to institute storage programs. These were not cheap, either. But they did less to enrich even the rich farmers than they did to enrich the companies that employed the cadres of World War II veterans-turned-organization men. Daniel (2009) notes:

> In 1959, the USDA issued a report on recipients of storage payments in excess of $500,000 to handlers of grain, rice, and cotton. The C-G-F Grain Company of Fort Worth headed the list with $14.8 million, with Cargill close behind at $13.2 million. The Federal Compress & Warehouse Company of Memphis received $4.4 million with the Panhandle Compress & Warehouse Company of Lubbock taking in $1.1 million. In 1955, Federal

Compress had received almost $11 million. In 1958, the Rice Growers Association of California received $871,637 and the Arkansas Rice Growers Cooperative $826,133. Even the storage of butter, cheese, and milk cost nearly a million dollars in 1958.

Double-dipping for bureaucrats and agribusiness

The Greediest, never ones to allow an unfortunate fact to stand in the way of increasing their wealth, ignored the ability of the USDA to reduce acreage planted via the Soil Bank program, while at the same time spending money at land grant universities where scientists were working on increasing yield per acre; this combination of mutually exclusive goals and funding for them was making the USDA inordinately powerful. The USDA, says Daniel (2009), "sought to please both the farmer and the processor, the growers and the companies that sold machines and chemicals, the scientists who increased production and the companies that stored the surplus." Who did they not seek to please? The consumer. But, to the "Corporation Man" Greeder, consumers — people — simply paled in comparison to progress and profit.

One of the USDA critics Daniel (2009) quoted said that the contradicting powers of the USDA were more harmful to Tennessee than the Civil War had been.

Chemicals, the jewels in the crown

In fact, the harm had hardly begun. In the 1960s, despite the surpluses and the Soil Bank, the USDA and its scientists and administrators, not to mention its marketing wizards, insisted that increasing production was essential to the nation's survival.

"Were farmers forced to give up chemicals, they warned, the country faced starvation."(Daniel 2009)

Deadly insecticides, proudly invented in Nazi Germany

Chemicals were a byproduct of World War II. DDT and 2,4-D were two of these, kept on the market even after they had been found to cause harm to wildlife and humans, and despite the warning by author Rachel Carson in her world-changing book, *Silent Spring*. While there were many exciting developments connected with World War II, chemicals got little play simply because they were not nearly as exciting as an atomic bomb.

Whatever chemicals were not home-grown were the spoils of war. It didn't occur to U.S. scientists, overjoyed to find captured German scientific records intact, that the organophosphates and nerve gases the Germans had developed might be less than desirable in a society that didn't want to kill people, considering the Germans' other experiments and the reason they developed the compounds in the first place. (Daniel 2009)

The German records led to the development of parathion, malathion and TEPP, plus 2,4-D, "an herbicide that in effect caused plants to grow themselves to death." This seems quite consistent with the tenor of most of the German experiments, that is, monstrous. What is unfortunate is that, as Daniel notes, "In post-war America, the fight against foreign enemies quickly became syntactically fused to the struggle against insects and weeds." (Daniel 2009)

One might also wonder if there is any connection between 2,4-D and increasing cancer rates. That antibiotics have escaped into the environment, with adverse impact on humans and animals, it would seem reasonable to assume that, for example, 2,4-D had, and was causing certain cells to grow themselves to death.

Pesticide residue of DDT, and more

The handy chemicals were touted by the USDA as safe for humans; the USDA neglected to mention that the same chemicals had poisoned acres and acres of ground in a failed attempt to eliminate fire ants. The USDA also failed to mention the presence of the chemicals in milk. Indeed, "To hear the USDA tell it, the world had no decent food until the USDA began encouraging farmers to abandon centuries of effective husbandry practice in favor of a chemical feast." (Daniel 2009)

Chums on the road to agribusiness happiness

Early on, W.L. Popham, an official of the USDA's research arm, the Agricultural Research Service, predicted that without chemicals, food production would fall and crops "would be of low quality and unwholesome because of worms and rot." (Daniel 2009) His fear-mongering was ratified by a USDA official who complained in 1969, after environmentalism had begun to attract followers, "Soon we may be without food if the nitrate and phosphate opponents have their way" (Popham 1969)

The folly of the USDA's ways wasn't long in making itself known. In October 1956, malathion sprayed to combat a fruit fly infestation "affected people with asthma and caused skin rashes."(Daniel 2009)

Daniel (2009) noted that, "A *Business Week* columnist reported in September 1957 that sixty persons near Glen Allan, a small

Mississippi community near Greenville, were ill with a fevers of 105 degrees and suffered from 'asthmatic breathing, various flu-like symptoms, and some pneumonia'." Dr. Mary Hogan, who treated the victims, announced that "spraying cotton fields with an insecticidal mixture" caused the outbreak. (Daniel 2009)

Whatever harm to small farms owned by African-Americans had been left undone in the farm policies wealth transfer scheme was completed by chemicals. At a time when black Americans were fighting for civil rights, they were even more uncomfortable seeking medical help locally. Often, they suffered and died from using the new agricultural chemicals without ever seeking medical help, Daniel notes.

It was likely that many didn't know why they were sick. As late as the mid-1960s, producers of agrichemicals often put no warnings on their package and offered no antidotes on their labels.

The annals of the suffering caused by the chemicals is extensive, not only in the South, but throughout the nation. Daniel provides sufficient examples to make his case that the chemicals were debilitating and/or deadly, and the chemical manufacturers had no intention except to expand their use, regardless of their effect on those working with the chemicals, or on the agricultural products that would eventually land on consumer tables. And land they did, on the Formica-topped monstrosities at which most Baby Boomers spent dinner hour night after night, eating fruits and vegetables coated with pesticide residues, eating milk with residues lurking within, and meat that came with a full complement of warmed-over pollutants from organophosphates to nerve gas.

Remember who was in charge of all these programs at the time: the Greediest Generation. They forged blindly ahead, heedless of any possible ethical issues, ignorant even of the need to evaluate new products and systems for safety and efficacy before putting them to use. They remained studiously ignorant of the devastating effect the combination of land policies and chemical consumption was having on society in agricultural areas, and on the cities where they displaced farm workers ended up with time on their hands and unhappiness in their hearts. One thing they didn't ignore, however, was corporate profits.

The 1950s and 1960s was the era of the Corporation Man, the Man in the Gray Flannel Suit, the lockstep clone bought with a new car every other year, a house in the suburbs made possible by Levitt and Sons and President Dwight D. Eisenhower's Interstate Highway system, and a good start in life via the GI Bill, a leg up that far exceeded that of any previous or subsequent generation in the world.

Poisoning our land and air with chemicals

Almost nothing that happened in America in the years after WWII was devoid of some military influence, from the captured German scientific papers that helped us poison our land and air with chemicals, to the GI Bill that offered ex-servicemen (and a very few women) the education and housing that allowed them to earn enough early in life to overbreed. Even today's Internet began as a research project of the U.S. military, the Defense Advanced Research Projects Agency (DARPA), which, with Massachusetts Institute of Technology, developed the precursor of the Internet, called ARPANET, as early as 1962.

Just so, the development of the Interstate Highway system was based on the idea of President Dwight David Eisenhower that we needed good roads in the event of war, so that the military could quickly transport troops across the nation. There are two things wrong with this excuse:

- First, most nations attempt to make travel across their land mass difficult, knowing full well that an enemy on foreign shores will not know the landscape as well as natives and will thus move more slowly than natives no matter what; any foreign army would travel a well-paved, well-marked road if it were handed to them. To this day, people in Ireland misdirect road signs out of habit, a habit they learned during British occupation in order to delay troop arrival in Irish villages.

- Second, one of the main beneficiaries of the highway system was, not surprisingly, the auto industry. But it wasn't only the family car that drove the development of highways; it was the trucking industry. For example, it was during the Eisenhower administration that the pneumatic tubes that carried mail from post office to post office in New York City, Boston and Philadelphia were shut down. Opened in 1898, the tubes had been in service and working well except for a shutdown during World War I. As Robin Pogrebin noted in a *New York Times* article, "In New York City, because of the high population density and a great amount of lobbying from contractors, the tube system remained in operation until Dec. 1, 1953, when it was suspended pending a review. Later that month, the post office ended the contract."(Pogrebin 2010) It awarded contracts for new post office local and long-distance vehicles instead.

Two other side effects of the Federal-Aid Highway Act of 1956 (also known as the National Interstate and Defense Highways Act) were these: The path was opened for the commuter lifestyle and the ultimate destruction of inner cities (which are compact and efficient and relatively "green") in favor of suburbs (sprawling and wasteful; only the grass is "green"), and the constant search for oil, wars for oil and environmental destruction for oil all became not a possibility but a certainty.

Family farming laid to eternal rest

Because of the actions of the USDA, the food scientists, the conglomerate food processors and their unending drive to wring greater production from less land and effort (regardless of the healthfulness of either the end product or the farm and farm workers), and the marriage of refrigeration and highways, the Greediest were the last generation to be able to be small farmers.

In the United States, where the vast majority of people were farmers at the time of the American Revolution, fewer people are now (2010) full-time farmers (less than 1 percent of the population) than are full-time prisoners. (Halweil 2000)

Here are some other statistics that make it clear that farming as a life's work and as a way of life is something not to be passed on beyond the Greeder generation:

- More than half of all Japanese farmers were over 65 in 2000, meaning that they are about 75 now. Even if they have passed the farm on to a younger generation, it's still meaningful that half of the farmers producing during the entire Baby Boom generation had come from a small generation, and the other half was drawn from the two subsequent small generations. (Halweil 2000)

- In 2000, it was projected that fifty percent of farms would go out of business in the subsequent decade. (Halweil 2000)
- In New Zealand, 40 percent of all dairy farms were expected to disappear between 2010 and 2015. (Halweil 2000)

Perhaps the most frightening statistic was this one: "In the U.S. states of Nebraska and Iowa, between a fifth and a third of farmers are expected to be out of business within two years." (Halweil 2000) That would have happened by 2002. Doubtless, by the depths of the recession that began in 2008 before George W. Bush left office, there were far fewer farms than that.

Between the destruction of the small farm by the USDA's efforts, the development of chemicals that kill insects and parasites while poisoning the land and the food itself, and the construction of a highway system that was a boon to large, fleet-owning businesses and big oil, it is almost inevitable that farming would follow widget-making into mass production. Not only that, but the new breed of factory (that is to say corporate) farmers had a useful philosophy at their beck and call, one that would justify inhumanity and maximize profits all in one go.

Animals no different than a pile of stones

Beyond the logistical and mechanical, scientific and engineering reasons for the rise in factory farming, the Greediest' desire to live better for less — despite having more children than any generation in history and living farther from each other and commercial centers than ever in history — is firmly at the center of all those ancillary reasons for the development of the factory farm. Some credit must also be given to the philosopher Descartes who opined that animals were no different than a pile of stones and did not feel pain and therefore did not need for us to act humanely toward them, a belief now almost as widely rejected as the idea that the sun revolves around the earth. Except, of course, it has not been rejected by the Greediest when if fits with their overwhelming desire to have whatever they want, whatever the price because…well, because they fought in World War II.

Author Darien Ibrahim has investigated the issue of the rise of factory farms over the past 50 years, and "attributes the rise of factory farms to consumer demand for low-cost meat, eggs, and dairy, as well as animals' legal classification as property, which permits their ownership by corporations. For animals, factory farms are dreadful; for corporations and consumers, they are beneficial. The efficiencies of factory farms enable both rich and poor consumers to afford meat and corporations to profit from selling more of it. This creates a chasm between what we now say about how animals should be treated, as sentient beings, and how we actually treat them."(Ibrahim 2007, 89+)

Using chickens as an example, Ibrahim traces the rise of factory farming via vertical integration. Before the 1920s, most chickens were used for egg production and, moreover, were raised on family farms. Most farms, he noted, had about 23 chickens, enough to produce eggs for family use and some for sale, and chickens for the family to eat, eventually. However, those farms also grew vegetables that had to be marketed locally and quickly before they spoiled. In the 1920s, farmers in Delmarva, a region of Delaware, Maryland and Virginia, decided they could market chickens in the nearby large markets of Washington, DC, Baltimore, Philadelphia, New York and even Boston.

During World War II, when the military commandeered most beef and pork, the sale of "broilers" increased to make up the difference in domestic diets. Notes Ibrahim, "...after World War II, integrated poultry companies came to own or control every part of the production cycle," including flocks, maturing chickens, warehousing and distribution, advertising, sales, processing and by-products. "As early as 1963, the *Wall Street Journal* reported, 'Nearly 95% of commercial broilers are now produced under the management of business organizations which own or control some combination of hatcheries, feed mills, processing plants, marketing services and research facilities...'." (Sawyer 1971, 1776-177.)

While it hasn't gotten any better, a handful of concerned citizens are trying to return to traditional American farming techniques, in which crops and animals are treated to the best husbandry practices. Plants are given natural nutrients; animals are fed naturally and allowed to wander as nature intended until they are needed for food. But the USDA, no longer the farmer's friend if it ever was and certainly not the consumer's, is putting up roadblocks of the sort only big agribusiness can surmount.

An article published by the conservative *National Review* in 2003 noted that only two percent of American farms were organic,[10] hardly a major threat to agribusiness. But any threat to the status quo is taken very seriously by the food conglomerates

---

[10] Recall, less than one percent of all US farms are family farms; while conglomerates can engage in organic farming, most organic farms appear to be family farms, meaning the number of organic farms is almost infinitesimally small.

and, since they have the lobbying power and organic producers don't, guess who wins?

Among the biggest roadblocks to improved farming practices and improved foods for the consumer are those concerning slaughter of animals.

The Midwest's lock on killing animals

Animal slaughter must be done in USDA-approved facilities. Unfortunately, these are not liberally spread around the nation, but rather are located at the big centrally located Midwestern feedlots where truckload after truckload of protein on the hoof arrives from conglomerates. A small organic producer, slaughtering only 200 animals a year, cannot hope to afford the feed-lot/slaughter process Big Ag has perfected (if one wants to call it that).

Few small producers could afford the minimal facilities USDA requires if they wanted to build their own. Jenny Drake owns of Peaceful Pastures, a farm raising free-range beef, pork, turkey, veal, lamb, goat, duck and chicken without hormones and antibiotics (standard "additives" in factory farming, with the hormones implicated in too-early maturation of girls and antibiotics implicated in the growth of resistant bacteria, not to mention the effects of antibiotics in streams and their effects on fisheries). Drake looked into starting a small processing facility, which she could have built for about $20,000. However, to meet USDA requirements, that facility would also have needed an inspector's office, a private and separate phone line, a paved parking lot, and handicapped accessible bathrooms. Says Drake, "We have to meet the same physical standards as a Tyson's, and we just can't do it." (Dreher 2003)

Fast Food Nation: **Big ag's lock on US food and US health**

No one wants to let just anyone kill animals and sell meat at the roadside. However, organic producers regulated in some way and selling food locally — thus avoiding the storage and shipping problems that can lead to spoiled food — would seem to be at least as good a bet as Big Ag. The *National Review* article noted:

> Besides the issue of antibiotics and hormones, there's the more serious matter of food-borne pathogens and food-borne illness. In the best-selling book *Fast Food Nation*, Eric Schlosser argues that factory-farming livestock in overcrowded, diseased feedlots and the rapid, assembly-line processing of meat through a handful of slaughterhouses before dispersing it throughout the country create ideal conditions for mass spreading of contamination. (Dreher 2003)

Regulating local organic meat producers is one possibility. Another is mobile slaughtering facilities. Neither has gained much momentum. However, "As one rural-affairs expert told the *New York Times* recently: 'We give a lot of tax breaks and direct payments to big agriculture companies that don't do much for the local economy, but rarely do we give anything to the little guy trying to start a business and stay in town'."(Dreher 2003)

Those little guys? Right. They are Baby Boomers and children of Baby Boomers. But the Greediest Generation's Big Ag — grown up into self-perpetuating bureaucracies — has the Boomers all lined up for the slaughter.

CHAPTER FIVE: IMMIGRATION POLICY AS A FULL-EMPLOYMENT TOOL FOR THE GREEDIEST

Many Americans are phobic about immigration, an odd stance for a nation founded by immigrants and the offspring of immigrants. The 2010 draconian move by Arizona to make it doubly illegal to be an illegal immigrant, and a bit dicey even for legal ones and for non-immigrants of dark complexion and eyes and hair, purported to be about saving American jobs. Some said it was about racism. It was probably about both, and about the expediency built into the culture by the needs of the Greediest.

After the riots after WWI, it is understandable that the fathers of the Greediest wanted to prevent a recurrence, and therefore wanted to protect jobs, the issue in those early protests. But by introducing the concept of immigration reform — that is, limits — to the Greediest, a dangerous "circle up the Cadillacs" mindset was established, one picked up in 2010 and carried toward the goal of a dumbed down, tarted up, woefully insular and wickedly chauvinistic America by Jan Brewer, governor of Arizona, and a member of Brokaw's generation. She and her minions enacted a law that, in essence, would make it doubly illegal to be illegal, as if being illegal wasn't frightful enough for an impoverished Mexican looking for a job, any job, any pay, any way.

Brewer is the offspring of a long line of circle-up-the-Cadillacs politicians, a true torch-bearer for the Greeders who preceded her. They were more effective, however, and a lot less controversial. After all, they did not have ageing Boomers around to point out the inhumanity of their ways.

In 1944, congressional nativists "proposed several bills to suspend all immigration to ensure domestic jobs for returning servicemen."(Tichenor 2002, 177) A coalition of humanitarian groups, including the American Jewish Committee (AJC), Hebrew Immigrant Aid Society (HIAS), B'nai B'rith, the National Catholic Welfare Conference, the Federal Council of Churches, the American Committee for Christian Refugees, the American Civil Liberties Union (ACLU), the Common Council for American Unity, and the Young Women's Christian Association (YWCA), all tried to mobilize liberal forces to combat the isolationist, protectionist mood of Congress.

The efforts of these groups were likely to be heard and heeded by a succession of post-war presidents, Truman, Eisenhower, Kennedy, and Johnson, who "would serve as a powerful institutional champion of expansive immigration reform in the post-war decades." (Tichenor 2002, 178)

Those presidents were likely responding, as well, to the Cold War need to acquire upper-level immigrants who might come bearing secrets useful to national security, and to appear, in the eyes of the global community, to be the generous, expansive opposite of the inward-looking, consistently threatening Soviet Union. But there had also been a sea change in the character of the office of president.

In Washington's day, the president had been a person of civic virtue, according to observer John White. (Tichenor 2002, 179) Beginning with Truman's decision to drop nuclear weapons on Japan, the office of president had metamorphosed into commander-in-chief, a viewpoint many were (and still are) inclined to hold regarding not only presidential war-making powers, but presidential powers over all aspects of international contact. This, notes David J. Tichenor, author of *Dividing Lines: The Politics of Immigration Control in America,* (Tichenor 2002, 179) put the newly defined Leader of the Free World above mere politics. It allowed the president greater latitude in what he wanted to do, and how he went about doing it, with less demur from Congress than might formerly have been experienced. It allowed what the late Howard Zinn had referred to as the "cowardly action" of dropping nuclear bombs on Hiroshima and Nagasaki.

Humanitarianism had nothing to do with Greeder immigration law

It was not for humanitarian reasons that each of these presidents sought expanded immigration. Rather, "they resented quotas that sometimes prevented admitting those escaping Communist regimes. Post-war presidents responded by calling for major immigration reform and by taking independent executive action to provide relief to refugees outside the dictates of existing legal restrictions." (Tichenor 2002, 180)

Tichenor also noted that they feared being tarred with the racism brush if they held to the national origin quotas that had been in place throughout the 1920s and 1930s. They regarded opening immigration as an imperative for supporting the moral leadership of the United States in world opinion. In this regard, these presidents were in tune, early on, with the increasingly expansive attitudes toward the world's peoples found in the Baby Boom. Regardless, they had to bend to the wishes of the US Congress, which remains, to this day, the philosophical progeny of the reactionary elements that built the post-war cocoon for returning soldiers, and those soldiers who never saw any reason whatever to share the largesse they had received with others.

In the issue of immigration during the administrations of presidents Truman through Johnson, the reactionary cohort usually won the day. While presidents pushed for opening the immigration floodgates, McCarthyites in congress were infinitely more cautious, fearing that members of an international communist conspiracy would take advantage of the opportunity. A coalition of conservative Republicans and Southern Democrats managed to have immigration legislation enacted in the early 1950s that reaffirmed quotas, despite the humanitarian lobbying of so many well-regarded organizations.

While presidents continued to want to expand immigration, Tichenor noted that "most Americans opposed any increase in immigrant admissions" as late as 1964; in short, the Congress the Greediest elected was indeed acting in response to what the Greediest, rewarded with a tight labor market and unwilling for anyone else to have a bit of their prosperity, wanted. Indeed, in 1945, when Truman had succeeded in extending special relief to Europe's displaced persons, a Gallup poll "suggested that most Americans were unsympathetic to Europe's dispossessed: 51 percent of those polled favored a decrease or suspension of immigration, 32 percent supported the policy status quo, and a mere 5 percent approved of increases in immigration. *Veterans and members of labor unions were among the most staunchly restrictionist respondents.*" (Emphasis added)
(Tichenor 2002, 182)

Cowardly liberators rather than larger-than-life heroes

It is difficult to connect this extremely anti-humane response with the generation has always claimed to have liberated Europe from Nazi power, saved many Jews in many lands, and kept the Pacific from becoming puppets of Hirohito, and continues — with the help of panderers such as actor Tom Hanks[11]— to successfully beat that drum. But think about this: The American soldiers who volunteered for World War II[12] were not fighting for the Jews or Europeans or residents of coconut-strewn atolls. They were fighting for two other reasons.

First, they were sent not to save the Jews, but to save a major ally, England. The United States was still living the Rooseveltian (Theodore) doctrine of walking softly but carrying a big stick; by saving tiny Britain, the U.S. retained an ally and strengthened its position in the Old World. This was, arguably, not done out of friendship or a feeling of global community. This nation had not embraced the League of Nations; we were still in a political infancy that regarded isolationism as the next best thing to world domination. Isolation with the undying gratitude of valuable Western nations would be that much better than isolation by itself.

The soldiers of World War II fought not to preserve Europe and the Pacific, but to extend America. War-ravaged Britain, the

---

[11] Hanks is an actor. He played roles of soldiers in WWII. He also played the role of a hippie-era Peace Corps volunteer. Why he should become the mouthpiece of the greediest generation rather than his own is difficult to fathom. Actors, in political settings, should be seen and not heard. Ronald Reagan is the foremost example of this.

[12] Recall, the percentage of draftees in WWII was higher than in Vietnam; there were also more anti-war protests than there were about Vietnam.

nation that spawned the US, was the logical place to do it. Thus, the inhumane immigration attitude of Congress is, in fact, perfectly consistent with the military service the Greediest had rendered during the war. It was narrowly self-serving and *un*generous to a fault.[13]

Second, joining up was popular (but not that popular, see below) both because of the recruiting efforts of the U.S. military, which touted the patriotism, the *manliness*, of it, and because before the war, jobs were still in short supply. As a result, via a single action — joining up — a young man got to feel larger than life, and send some money home to Mom. What's not to like, if you're a man of 17 or 18 or 20, and the idea of a Polynesian atoll beats pumping gas for Old Man Gotrocks for a small wage and no glory, and living the quiet life at home with Mom, Dad and Sis? Besides which, The Greediest did not sign up as avidly as the Greatest Generation myth would have one believe. While 2/3 of the soldiers in Vietnam (contrary to popular belief) were volunteers, 2/3 of the soldiers serving in WWII had to be drafted. (McCaffrey 1993)

Still, what Congress wrought, the grunts of World War II not only embraced, but nurtured. After the war, back home and voting, nothing changed. The McCarran-Walter Act (Immigration and Nationality Act, or INA) of 1952 included draconian limits on all immigration except that from northern and western Europe, and on anyone considered by government functionaries to be un-American; the list included many authors (even some from basically acceptable Britain) as well as Pierre

---

[13] Even the command on the ground in England was stingy. While US troops and fliers had abundant rations, the British troops and fliers—who were among the bravest in the world anywhere—had very little...and the US did not share. Except, of course, chocolates and hosiery when the troops wanted to appeal to a local female.

Trudeau before he became Canadian Prime Minister. Once he was the leader of our closest English-speaking neighbor he was, despite his somewhat suspect French surname and his former un-American activities, acceptable to the masses, or at least, the politicians they had elected were willing to take the chance of welcoming him.

President Truman, not being a military man, considered the immigration bill to be antediluvian, a slap in the face to those who believed the United States had been chosen to lead a new sort of global community that was more tolerant of differences than any before. Congress overrode his veto. No, Congress said, we were still the nation of Teddy Roosevelt, chosen to lead by might and not right. Now, the U.S. didn't even walk softly. But the stick, beating the rest of the globe into the form we desired, was bigger than ever, wielded by a Congress beginning to be run by and for the Greediest Generation as their parents — the WWI generation that had taken such good care of them — retired.

While the Greediest were quite willing to congratulate themselves on liberating Europe and the Pacific, they were quite *unwilling* to accept those they had liberated as equals and compatriots. It was an added benefit for them that, during their prime earning years from 1945 through 1965, their jobs and incomes were protected, and the opportunity to gain wealth all but assured.

The Conscience of the Senate: Good intentions, bad result for Boomers

In 1965, the Hart-Celler Act (Immigration and Nationality Act of 1965) wildly expanded immigration. The act was proposed by

Rep. Emanuel Cellar (D-NY) and co-sponsored by Sen. Philip Hart (D-MI), and was supported by Sen. Ted Kennedy (D-MA.) Note that both sponsors and the big-gun supporter were from heavily industrial states that also had extensive higher education systems.

Celler was born in 1888, and was too old for WWII service. Celler was of the generation that took such pains to care for the GIs; the fact that he was Jewish and could gain votes in his district by rewarding servicemen and opening doors to more Jewish immigration was probably not an insignificant incentive.

Philip Hart served in WWII and was wounded during the Normandy invasion. He was known as the "conscience of the Senate," a sobriquet which accords well with sponsorship of what could be seen as a humanitarian bill. The only reason it was not humanitarian in effect, although perhaps in intent, was that it formed another nail in the coffin the Greediest were thoughtlessly (or possibly with malice) constructing for their own children's futures.

Sen. Ted Kennedy was born in 1932, making him a member of the Silent Generation. Regardless of his personal foibles, Kennedy maintained integrity regarding humanitarian and egalitarian ideals during his entire congressional career, fighting until literally his last breath to give Americans in the 21st century the minimal humanitarian benefits Europeans had enjoyed for well over half a century.

When is enough not enough? When we're talking about the Greediest

In some ways — ways all geared toward Greeder welfare — it was just as well the coalition of three generations enacted the 1965 immigration law, as Congress was about to do something else that would demand, in future, lots and lots of warm, working, tax-paying bodies.

In 1965, the Greeder Congress enacted a universal, single-payer healthcare plan for retirees which, added to the Social Security invented to save their parents from the workhouse, would ensure that the Greediest Generation was the first one to experience a better life in their old age than during their prime (or at least, not one wildly diminished, as in the pre-Social Security past) without their having to provide Dollar One for themselves. Why should they? They could saddle their kids with their upkeep, and they could do it to a much, much greater degree than FDR could have imagined when Social Security itself was enacted.

At the same time, the Greediest ensured penury for their offspring at retirement, even before George Bush's financial meltdown. While The Greediest mainly had company pensions in addition to Social Security, they enacted the legislation permitting Keoghs and IRAs, effectively allowing corporations not to create pension funds and "allowing" workers coming into the workforce — Boomers — to manage their own retirement funding. Naturally, the word "allow" is used tongue-in-cheek. It forced them to; however, since their payroll taxes kept increasing for the Greediest' Social Security, it was more difficult for them to save than it had been for their parents who did get company pensions. In addition, wages became flat in about 1974, making it harder still.

Social Security was meant as a safety net in a changing society. Medicare was far, far more. Medicare was a springboard for a level of wealth transfer unimaginable before the Greeder Congress of the early 1960s decided to mortgage the futures of its children and grandchildren and turn the United States into a partial socialist society, with only one segment the beneficiaries of that social engineering, the Greediest.

Teabaggers: Legitimate offspring of the Greediest

It must be added — and added forcefully: those same Greeders decried loud and long the socialism from which they so greatly benefit. Note, too, that their spear-carrying progeny, the teabaggers who emerged during the presidency of the first black man to hold the office, were also mainly retired people in 2008 and 2009, meaning they are *not* the Baby Boomers they've claimed to be, but rather members of the Silent Generation.

The Silent Generation, by and large, carries the same mental attitudes of the Greediest; rarely, they have broken out. But their generational breakouts were, without doubt, sparks for many of the more liberal Boomer attitudes. Bob Dylan, for example, is a member of the Silent Generation, as was the late comedian George Carlin. Those artists and several others like them were just enough older than the Boomers, thank goodness, to be effective in speaking to the Boomers. And it should be added, regarding Dylan, Carlin, et al, the Greediest hated them as thoroughly as it despises the Boomers who poked fun at their elders, or turned popular culture away from the saccharine melange of the post-war era. Ozzy Osbourne, David Letterman and more.

As a result of the new demands for unearned currency to support retired folks, it became clear that, as heavily as they were willing to tax Boomers, more worker/taxpayers would be needed to finance Greeder retirement. What to do? Simple: Reverse the adamant anti-immigration stance that had existed while the Greediest were establishing careers, and throw open the doors of America to the world. Greeder Bonus: Third-world immigrants tend to breed early and often, adding even more bodies to do the work to keep the Greediest in their accustomed style.

So, once again, the McCarran-Walter Act was a boon to the Greediest.

By 1965, the Greediest Generation had had two decades of increasing prosperity. They had expanded their Levittown homes or had traded up. They had lots of children to support them in their old age, and they had ever-increasing payments from Social Security. Medicare, to ease their health worries, had been established. What was there for a person to desire?

More. The Greediest wanted more.

Open the immigration floodgates, drown Boomers

In the early 1960s, annual immigration stood at about 300,000, seemingly sufficient to shift low-paying jobs to people who wanted freedom more than they wanted cash. Immigration reform in 1965, however, spelled increases that were truly significant compared to the U.S. population *in situ*. From 1966-1989—the years when the Baby Boom was finishing its education, returning from a hopeless Asian war, and trying to find a couple of decades to gain some economic security as its parents had been able to do — immigration grew to 12 million, almost five percent of the US population as enumerated in the 1990 census. "The average annual number of immigrants admitted during this period of 24 years was 506,927, which was about 2.4 times as large as the number of 214,144 for the period of 1921-1965." (Yang 1995, 18) Note: In real terms, it was more

like five times as large a number, as the earlier period was
nearly twice as long.

These numbers for new workers in the United States are, in fact,
low; illegal immigration is not taken into account.

By 1990, when Baby Boomers might have been enjoying the
prospect of some money to spend and an empty nest around the
corner, the foreign-born population of the nation was 7.9
percent, meaning several things, none of them conducive to
Baby Boom wealth building. For example:

- It meant that the Baby Boom's own children, a baby bust
  in comparison to the Boom, would be almost as
  pressured to find good jobs as Boomers had been; many
  would never leave home or would start returning to the
  nest after leaving and finding the real world was a lot
  more difficult than indulgent Boomer parents had led
  them to believe. And that was before the Greeder global
  financial meltdown, engineered by New World Order
  Führer George H.W. Bush and carried out by his
  mentally feeblest (and thus most biddable) son, George
  W.
- It signalled growing demands on infrastructure.
- It signalled growing demands on entitlements, without
  the preceding contributions to the national tax coffers to
  offset that drain.

Further, European prosperity during the period meant more
immigrants came from South America and Asia simply because
Europeans were fat and happy at home. This meant more
problems integrating immigrants into what is still a European-
based, English-speaking U.S. society. There were language
issues larger and more intransigent among less-well-educated

South Americans than those presented by the linguistically more sophisticated Europeans. (The Asians, with a cultural love of learning, arguably had almost as little trouble with the language as Europeans did.)

The lower level of education among the bulk of the new immigrants than there had been in the European immigration just before and just after World War II, when large numbers of immigrants had been highly educated Jews, making almost immediate contributions and requiring little, caused demands for change in US society that the Greeders, above all, resented, although they had been the authors of the problem in the first place.

If you doubt this, consider the sudden demand that Spanish become virtually a second language in America. Had this happened for Gaelic-speaking Irish? For Italians? For Germans? For European Jews? No. All those groups were literate in their native tongues, by and large, and while learning English might have been taxing, it was not impossible. Moreover, because the European immigrants were broke, but not poor, they expected to have to work hard — at jobs and at language and culture — to make the life they wanted. They had the cultural and educational tools to do so; the bulk of the Hispanic immigration did not. Among the most vocal element against bi-lingualism was the Greeder generation; indeed, look to Arizona and Gov. Jan Brewer's draconian anti-Mexican legal maneuvers for proof. Is it jobs she's protecting? Arguably, but just as arguably, the entire exercise is one in anti-Hispanic prejudice.

The humanitarian response

One might be tempted to say, So what if the immigrants were untutored and unskilled? In a humanitarian sense, that's the proper response. But in a practical sense for the Baby Boom, the impact was enormous, and negative all around. That is, with the bulk of immigration being made up of uneducated people who taxed the infrastructure and contributed little in the way of taxes,[14] there was also a segment that was ready, able and willing to eat the rest of the Baby Boom's lunch: the influx of better-educated immigrants from China, Taiwan, India, the Philippines and Korea. Yang noted that large numbers of:

> ...scientists, engineers, doctors, nurses, postsecondary teachers, and other professionals, have made significant use of the occupational preference categories. Many of these immigrants were foreign students who adjusted to immigrant status. In addition, in 1981 Taiwan was recognized as an independent entity for immigration purposes and given a separate quota of 20,000. This doubled the quota of 20,000 available to 'China,' which had been previously shared by the People's Republic of China and Taiwan. (Yang 1995, 21)

Then an influx of educated workers occurred, due to the continuing tinkering with the 1965 immigration law changes, just when Baby Boomers needed to solidify their employment positions and seriously build for their own retirements. Between 1975 and 1985, Yang noted:

---

[14] They contributed little in income tax as many were illegal and worked off the books. Many working on the books sent more money home than they spent in the US, missing contribution to the economy through regressive taxation as well.

...nearly 600,000 Indochinese refugees from Vietnam, Laos, and Kampuchea were admitted. They became eligible for adjustment to permanent residence after two year's physical presence in the United States under the Indochinese Refugee Act of 1977 and the Refugee-Parolee Act of 1978. This largely explains the surge of Asian immigration since 1977. (22)

While they were not as educated as a group as the post-War European immigrants, they were industrious and eager to get ahead in an alien culture.

While it was humane to admit these refugees, considering it was the U.S. presence in their native region that had arguably expanded regional conflicts that might have had regional solutions without interference, its impact on the Baby Boom was enormous and negative. This wave of immigration diminished the numbers of jobs available to U.S. graduates, and depressed the salaries of the jobs that were available. In short, not only were U.S. Boomers required to compete with each other as they had since kindergarten; they now had to compete with the very people so many had lost life, limb and loved ones over in Vietnam, the Greeder's most useless war until now.[15]

Double the trouble for Boomers

The double threat to Boomer income, then, was that there were many more uneducated immigrants using services but contributing little; there were also many more well-educated

---

[15] Arguably, the Afghan and Iraqi wars of George W. Bush are even more useless, except of course for the oil to be had, something lacking in the Vietnam conflict. That does not, however, satisfy any sort of ethical argument over the value of Bush's wars.

immigrants taking good-paying jobs with which the Boomers might have earned enough to pay for the uneducated immigrants without losing their own prosperity.

As an additional burden, uneducated immigrants no longer sought settlement in rural areas where there was abundant farm work, a place where educated Boomers wouldn't be seeking work in great numbers. Farming had been mechanizing before WWII; after WWII, the excess vehicle manufacturing capacity had to be used somehow, and mechanized farm implements offered one major place to take up the slack. A company-run or –affiliated farm had access to capital and machinery; it did not need illiterate immigrants to house, clothe and feed to get the tomatoes harvested. By 1965, farming in America had gone a long way toward being the highly mechanized corporate entity it is today, offering little attraction to traditional agricultural workers. (Yang 1995, 22) And those were the least of its burgeoning problems for society.

The uneducated workers settled in cities, stressing the infrastructure, filling the schools, and taking the jobs Boomer children would need in order to pay for college since George W. Bush's NCLB, in concert with the Greediest' historic anti-education tax referendum "nay" votes, had fixed it so that the Boomers would be the last generation to enjoy almost adequate public education in America.

Offshoring is the ultimate immigration explosion

The penultimate chapter in the decimation (or worse) of the Baby Boom by the policies enacted by Reagan/Bush/Shrub Dubya did not appear until after 1998, which is when the cost of fiber optics plummeted. According to one source,(Granered 2005, 18) fiber optic capacity grew sevenfold between 2001 and

2003. When that happened, in addition to an influx of immigrants taking low-paying jobs, an outflux of much better-paying jobs occurred. The huge decline in fiber optic costs, and the installation of much more service, made it more cost effective to locate call centers in nations with lower employee costs, despite the costs associated with moving a business or a large part of a business across oceans, training staff and so on.

Indeed, while Mexican workers might temporarily take some low-level American jobs, and a few might even move up the ladder, outsourcing/offshoring ensures that the work will never return.

The Greediest eats the Boomers' brains

One might consider "offshoring" to be factory farming at its best. Why? Because the Greediest are literally eating the brains of the US workers being replaced. According to authors Ron Hira and Anil Hira, knowledge transfer generally precedes offshoring (which they call outsourcing). When the knowledge has been transferred, the US worker is laid off "after his or her knowledge has been extracted."(Hira and Hira 2005, 3) What's left is an empty desk in some cube farm in Omaha, a depressed laid-off worker, a suffering family…and more assurance that the income transfer engineered by the Greediest is working according to schedule. What schedule? The one that allows them to extract every bit of value before they die, leaving us to bury the husks and see what crumbs we might gather in order to carry on. Somehow.

CHAPTER SIX:
ENVIRONMENTAL ADVANCES RETRENCHED BY BOOMERS' LEAST MEMBER

Say what you will about the Baby Boom and the environment, a few facts are unavoidable. It was Boomers who celebrated the first Earth Day, and it is Boomers who are encouraging acceptance of the true meaning of dust to dust; green burials have been available since 1998, a time when the oldest Boomers began to take stock and realize that somehow, someday, their earthly remains would need to be dealt with.

While the Greediest developed an interest in cryogenics in the late 1960s[16]—aiming to stay around long enough for a cure for cancer to be found and reanimation techniques to be developed — the Boomers want, as they have since the beginning, to leave the earth without leaving behind a trail of debris.

By 2010, there were nine states willing to allow green burials, that is, burials without embalming fluid and containment in costly, non-biodegradable metal and concrete boxes. "That bucolic resting place we call a cemetery really functions more like a landfill," according to Mark Harris, author the 2007 book, *Grave Matters: A Journey Through the Modern Funeral Industry to a Natural Way of Burial*, as reported by Heather Whipps writing at LiveScience. (Whipps) Harris noted that enough metal is used for coffins and vault linings every year to "rebuild the Golden Gate Bridge."

---

[16] "The freezing of Dr. James Bedford in January 1967 was the first (albeit crude) cryonic suspension." Accessed at
http://www.alcor.org/Library/html/BedfordSuspension.html.

Harris also dispelled the belief that embalming is required. Not so, and, according the Centers for Disease Control, it offers no public health benefit.

Green cemeteries usually lack the "marble orchard" effect of the cemeteries lining so many public highways in the US. Rather, green cemeteries are likely to be wooded glades and the markers are often made of wood, or perhaps a small carved stone ...much as the household cat will be buried after he dies.

Whipps' article ended by suggesting such burials, costing a third of the usual price, might appeal to penny-pinching Boomers. True. But there are two ways to look at that:

- Either the appeal of green burial is consistent with the Boomer attempt to look after the earth and its people, or
- The Greediest have found the ultimate means of impoverishing their own children, and letting worms eat them while the Greediest repose like so many tacky pharaohs in tiny mausoleums, or expend even more earth energy keeping their useless bodies permanently on ice.

***

The first Earth Day happened on April 22, 1970. Its major proponent was Gaylord Nelson, a Democratic Senator from Wisconsin who had always been passionate about the environment. By birth date, 1916, he was a Greeder. By his actions, he was one of the few of that cohort worthy of the name Greatest. He also opened congressional inquiries into the safety of the birth control pill; the early versions were far more loaded with potentially harmful hormones than later ones, and there can be little doubt that improvements would have been slower were it not for his efforts. Nelson was also an avid proponent of small business, from which most new jobs arise, and a vocal opponent of Gerald Ford's candidacy as vice president.

In 1981, Nelson lost his seat. Rather than taking a highly paid, cushy job with a corporate lobbying organization or client, he became counselor for The Wildnerness Society. In 1995, he was awarded the Presidential Medal of Freedom by President Bill Clinton.

Indeed, Nelson stepped out of the Greeder mold, and Boomers can be glad he did. Despite the lobbying of the Boomers, intense in the late 1960s and early 1970s, it took a little help from inside government to move the environmental agenda ahead, after it had moved like the hands of a molasses clock in the arctic for the entirety of the 1950s and most of the 1960s.

The co-founder of Earth Day is Denis Hayes, born in 1944 and nominally a member of the Silent Generation. He was, however, a graduate student when he became Earth Day coordinator, and has worked in environmental causes ever since. Among his awards are the Jefferson Awards Medal for Outstanding Public Service, as well as awards from the Sierra Club, The Humane Society of the United States, the Natural Resources Council of America and the American Solar Energy Society. *Time* magazine named him Hero of the Planet in 1999.

Neither Hayes nor Nelson was awarded a Nobel Prize, despite international cooperation in Earth Day and the sea-change in awareness of the needs of the earth as well as its people that it spawned.

Environmental timeline, 1950s to now

There were few notable environmental steps forward in environmental issues in the 1950s. Indeed, the founding of The Nature Conservancy and passage of the Fish and Wildlife Act are among the few that pop up with any regularity in listings for the decade's milestones. Both of those are more concerned with a narrow band of activity, however, than what has developed as a cross-disciplinary approach to taking care of the earth.

In 1962, Rachel Carson's *Silent Spring* was published, and people began to notice what chemicals and buildings and waste disposal et al were doing to the natural world…and for the first time, considering that we actually do need the natural world in order to maintain a life-sustaining habitat on earth.

In 1962, Norman Borlaug — often credited as being the father of the "green revolution" — became the head of a wheat improvement program, for which read, early GM tinkering. The title Father of the Green Revolution persists, despite the fact that there is equally compelling evidence that Borlaug's tinkering and that of his successors is responsible for destruction of natural habitat when insects and animals find they cannot sustain their lives on unnatural foods to which millennia have NOT adapted them. Not to mention that we know very little about the long-term effects of eating "Dolly the Sheep" on humans.

Borlaug is credited with saving a million lives via his high-yield wheat. For that, he won the Nobel Peace Prize in 1970. One must wonder, however, how many millions will starve to death as a result of the franken-factory farming his tinkering with Mother Nature initiated. Indeed, this was amply chronicled by Alexander Cockburn in a *Sunday Business Post* article in 2003.

(Cockburn 2003) Because of Borlaug, factory farming was possible, indeed almost inescapable, which meant fewer family farms, employing family and some others. Factory farms are heavy on capital investment — tractors, plows, reapers, balers — because there are tax incentives for such investment, and because the hybrid, plasticized foodstuffs can be harvested cheaply with little human intervention in the form of farmers or farm workers.

It should surprise no one that a man who began as a chemist for DuPont should have developed products for Monsanto, a company amply and fairly criticized for widening social inequality in poor nations, destroying food distribution that had been improved only shortly before that via land reform, particularly in Central and South America. Unlike Nelson, Borlaug is an example of the worst excesses of ethically impoverished research undertaken time and again by Greeder scientists. On balance, Borlaug — careering willy-nilly toward a future all too likely to get out of control — is more a demon than a savior in environmental and nutritional terms.

Greeders' answer to everything: Mechanize and make it bigger

At roughly the time when Borlaug's juggernaut toward populating the fields and forests with mutant species was underway, protein stocks for many nations were compromised by decades of thoughtless overfishing of the worlds oceans. In 1969, summer-spawning herring stocks in Iceland collapsed due to overfishing and worsening environments, leaving only a small viable stock remaining in Norwegian coastal waters.

The Boomers did not cause that; policies of the Greediest did. Boomers were not in control of ocean fisheries in the 1960s; the Greediest were. Arguably, the Greeder inability to cooperate across national boundaries for the common good — but rather only for the gain of companies like Monsanto on land and their ocean-fishing counterparts reaping bounty from the oceans with no thought to the future — also helped to engineer the collapse.

In 1966, the US Congress enacted the National Wildlife Refuge System Act and the Fur Seal Act (an act which apparently had little impact on the thoughts or actions of Sarah Palin, fur-wearing, gun-toting Luddite opportunist governor of Alaska).

In 1969, the National Environmental Policy Act was passed.

Because only the earliest Boomers could have had an effect on policy in the mid- to late 1960s, they did get some help from some late Silent Generation members, such as Hayes, and even from some enlightened Greeders, such as Nelson. Of course, not all Boomers were equally environmentally conscious, just as not all the Greediest or Silents were environmentally ignorant. However, a look at a few more of the milestones points to increasing awareness as the Boomers became increasingly active, making it part of the Boomer legacy, and not the legacy, certainly, of the Greediest.

Highlights of modern American environmental actions

In 1970, the US Environmental Protection Agency was founded. Acts passed that year include the Clean Air Act and the Resource Recovery Act.

In 1971, Greenpeace was founded, but not in the US. It was founded in Vancouver, Canada, and has since expanded to offices in 41 nations.

In the US, the *Keep America Beautiful* campaign, featuring TV ads of a crying Indian, began.

In 1972, the Marine Mammal Protection Act, the Marine Protection, Research and Sanctuaries Act, the Noise Control Act, the Clean Water Act and the Coastal Zone Management Act were passed.

The year 1973 seemed fairly quiet, dealing much of the time with the OPEC oil embargo against the United States. A complete examination of that maneuver is a subject for a different book. Suffice it to say that, during the term of Richard Nixon in the White House, a great number of steps were taken by corporate entities globally to negate the effects of the "small is beautiful" and environmental movements increasingly appealing to Americans, and indeed to the global community.

In 1974, the first hint appeared that chlorofluorocarbons were causing the ozone layer to degrade.

Until the end of the 1970s, little additional environmental legislation was achieved. But in 1979, a wakeup call, in the form the Three-Mile Island Nuclear Plant leak, was sounded. Amazingly little resulted.

Between nuclear accidents (another major one occurred at Chernobyl, Ukraine, in 1986) and additional proof of a degrading ozone layer (meaning less protection from the sun's rays and earth's heating up as a result) and climate change, it should have been clear that more environmental research should be undertaken with more actions to follow as needed.

A new kind of date rape

Where were the Boomers who should have been pushing for it? Apparently, many of the earliest Boomers had voted for Ronald Reagan, and had become quiet about social issues in favor of making a buck. They forgot to mistrust anyone over 30 when they reached 30 themselves. For environmentalism, the 1980s were a lost decade; for Boomers, it was a time of lost focus, lost commitment, and one might even suggest, lost identity.

By 1997, however, it was clear that the US needed to rejoin the global community and join other nations in environmental work. The Kyoto Protocol, signed by most industrialized nations, bound signatories to committing to reducing emissions of carbon dioxide and five other "greenhouse gases." With Bill Clinton, the first Boomer president, holding the office for eight years and ending his terms with a budget surplus and personal ethics deficit, it seemed as if the Boomer generation might be making a comeback to fight for themselves, their offspring, their country and their planet.

But then, in the aftermath of the ludicrous and doubtless well-orchestrated Lewinsky affair[17]....

---

[17] One must recall the recruiting of Linda Tripp to spy on her friend and report it to her handlers. It would also be well to remember that she had worked for George H. W. Bush, and was retained by Bill Clinton...which should be a reminder to all new presidents to remove all the flunkies of their predecessors regardless of what supposed skills they bring to the job. Tripp's skills apparently included turning a dalliance into an almost disastrous matter of state, and profiting mightily out of it all.

And with the help of the United States Supreme Court, various law enforcement agencies in Florida, early computer voting in the Midwest...

With a Boomer cohort fragmented by disinterest in Al Gore (who seemed very tame next to Clinton)...

And an apparently continuing wish to have a chief executive who was an Everyman...

The Boomers drank the Rohypnol[18] served up by the Republicans. They went to sleep one night, and when they woke up, it appeared no one recalled being slipped a Mickey so they would forget how entertaining (in a good way) and effective Clinton had been and vote for his Number Two. Instead, they found that a seriously damaged boy toy, George W. Bush, had slipped between the sheets, and would shortly do what boy toys do between the sheets...all over them.

George W. Bush, the second Boomer president, represented the flip side of Bill Clinton. Where Clinton was brilliant and bigger than life, Bush was idiotic and paltry. Where Clinton actually identified with his cohort and with Americans generally, Bush identified only with the religious right, an apparent replacement for Brother Booze in his outer-directed, addicted life. Where Clinton followed the demands of logic (and sometimes political expediency), Bush followed the demands of Dick Cheney, and of his inner demons, crude little fellows not given to subtlety but rather to tantrum satisfaction on any number of fronts.

---

[18] Also called the "date rape" drug because those who ingest it cannot recall what happened to them in the previous few hours.

First hints that the second Boomer president was a throwback

With the anti-Boomer at the helm, then, it is no wonder that, in 2001, the United States rejected the Kyoto Protocol. President George W. Bush, born in 1946, had brought environmental ignominy to his generational cohort, in this and in every other environmental action his administration took. It is, in retrospect, little wonder that Generation Y, especially, blames Boomers for all the current ills in the world.

However, just as Gaylord Nelson was an almost singular Greeder, George W. Bush was an almost singular Boomer. The man from whom Bush, commander-in-thief, had stolen the presidency had been, in fact, awarded a Nobel Peace Prize in 2006 for his efforts against the global warming that Bush claimed didn't exist, despite heat waves and droughts unprecedented in recent times, and resulting deaths of millions.

Although an ally, and some would say sycophant, of George W. Bush, Britain's Prime Minister, Tony Blair, that same year described scientific evidence of global warming as overwhelming and noted that unchecked, the consequences would be disastrous.

Among Boomer voices at the top, George W. was deservedly alone, spouting his warmed-over Greeder idiocies to anyone who would listen. Thankfully, sufficient Boomers were sick of the quintessential anti-Boomer by 2008 to elect Barack Obama.

Unfortunately, in mid-2010, Mr. Obama had discarded very few of Greeder Wannabe Bush's execrable "environmental" programs and executive orders. (Note: Greeder Wannabe Bush would work as his monogram just as well as his given name.)

Selected highlights of Bush's environmental disasters

The following were collected by the National Resources Defense Council (NRDC), and can be found in full, along with many more, on their website.

2001
Cheney's National Energy Plan expedites drilling for natural resources on public lands, including the Arctic National Wildlife Refuge and the western Arctic.

Feb. 2002
Bush's Clear Skies plan is announced, meaning that an additional 79 million tons of coal could be burned by 2020, and making a mockery of the term clear skies. But he probably thought it sounded like bona fide environmentalism, as found in the Clean Air Act.

May 2002
Here's a thought: Let's store nuclear wastes inside a mountain in an earthquake zone. Let's gerrymander the boundaries of the Yucca Mountain nuclear storage site in order to meet Safe Drinking Water Act standards after the EPA shoves all that nuclear stuff down there.

Sept. 2002
How forgetful can one be? This forgetful: "For the first time in six years, the EPA omits global warming from its annual air pollution report." (NRDC 2010)

Nov. 2002
"The Bush administration allows oil drilling in Padre National Park, home to 11 endangered species and host to 800,000 tourists annually." (NRDC 2010) This is because Bush can count to ten, so eleven must be "a lot." And the tourist number just sounds big. So he can claim to have done this for all Americans.

On opening old toxic sites, creating new ones

April 2003
Not   surprisingly,   considering   its fundamentalist/Republican/creationist ethos, Utah cuts a deal with the Secretary of the Interior to allow oil and gas drilling in its wilderness, millions of acres of its wilderness.

Sept. 2003
There's only one way to say this, flat out, as NRDC did: "The EPA lifts a 25-year ban on the sale of land contaminated with PCBs, a chemical linked to neurological problems and cancer in humans, thereby opening more than 1,000 toxic sites to 'economic redevelopment'." (NRDC 2010)

Oct. 2003
While the nation gets upset at the antics of Mama Grizzly Sarah Palin, Bush had already trashed much of the Alaskan wilderness without her assistance. His administration exempted Alaska's Tongass rainforest from rules protecting national forests from development. In Sept. 2010, the Obama administration had not yet

overturned Bush's decision; recent federal management decisions have used it to justify opening more wilderness areas to timber sales and logging roads." (NRDC 2010)

Formaldehyde: Now it's toxic, now it ain't

May 2004
Apparently honoring Bush's weird science, the EPA Air Office decided that formaldehyde was only one ten-thousandth as toxic as people had thought it was a day earlier, and for decades before that.

Some editorializing is irresistible here: So which set of scientists — those who think formaldehyde is very, very toxic, or those who think it's about as toxic as distilled water — are the idiots? I know which one gets my vote, on the basis of prudence alone. But then Greeder Wannabe Bush was never much for prudence. Or real science.

Oct. 2004
Bush's administration altered news releases about climate change and kept the public in the dark about the dangers of global warming, according to NASA's top climate expert.

Dec. 2004
Anyone for a swim? "The EPA moves to finalize a policy that would release inadequately treated sewage into waterways as long as it is diluted with treated sewage, a process the agency calls 'blending'." (NRDC 2010)

One must wonder how blended such non-biodegradable solids as hypodermic needles might become. And one wonders how many parts per million of blended sewage is OK to swim in, or to eat fish from.

March 2005

"The New York Times finds more than 200 instances in which television stations aired videos by the EPA as *actual news."* (NRDC 2010)

Is this news? Yes. People consider the New York Times to live up to its motto, All the news that's fit to print. That tripe wasn't fit to print. So why did they print it? Only your lobbyist knows for sure.

Katrina: A cruel response worthy of a Greeder, and other watery matters

Oct. 2005

Whoever didn't die as a result of Bush's malfeasance regarding Katrina still has a chance to die, even now!

"In the aftermath of Hurricane Katrina, EPA data reveal the presence of toxic levels of lead and arsenic in family lawns and soil. As of 2008, the administration had not cleaned up the toxic soil." (NRDC 2010)

March 2006

"The EPA proposes weakening the method for calculating health standards for drinking water in small communities. The new rule would allow small water systems to exceed federal drinking water standards yet still label the water as 'protective of health'." (NRDC 2010)

I wonder what strip of federal land they will build the New Ministry of Truth upon. There is a movement to make cities more desirable, in terms of centrally locating jobs and services and minimizing commutes. But one might think dissuading people from living in rural towns because their drinking water was substandard might be counterproductive. It all hinges, then, on convincing people that "dirtier than a city's" is the equivalent of "protective of health."

Winning the death-penalty sweepstakes…again

2007
In the year 2007, the Bush administration broke its own record for granting oil and gas drilling permits on public land with a grand total of 7,124. It was probably difficult for wildlife to find a perch or a lair that wasn't a metal pipe.

Still, this should not be surprising; Bush's tenure as governor saw more people subjected to capital punishment than any other state in the nation. On average, Texas put someone to death every two weeks during Bush's term.

At least his death-dealing ways were consistent across species.

March 2007

"President Bush takes grizzly bears off the endangered species list, opening the door for the loss of bear habitat and increasing the potential for conflicts between bears and humans." (NRDC 2010)

Idiot.

April 2007

"The Supreme Court rules that CO2 meets the legal definition of a 'pollutant' under the Clean Air Act, rejecting President Bush's declaration of March 2001." (NRDC 2010)

Censored: Bush puts truth under wraps. Again.

Oct. 2007

"The Bush administration censors major sections of the Centers for Disease Control and Prevention's congressional testimony on the public health impacts of global warming, including the statement that it represents 'a serious public health concern'." (NRDC 2010)

Censorship? In Bush's United States? No.......

Jan. 2008

Bush's executive order of the day helped the US Navy circumvent a federal court's ruling that limited use of high-intensity radar off the coast of California.

Sonar disrupts the communication systems of dolphins and whales, both of which are often found off that coast.

U.S. submarines are found there, too, ostensibly looking for enemy subs — perhaps from such military powerhouses as, umm, Tonga. China is no longer the red menace, but rather the red consumer market; no danger there. Granted, North Korea is hostile and owns subs and could approach that coast. Frankly, the likelihood of North Korea getting in range with or without sonar seems as likely as Paris Hilton developing a working set of ethical and behavioral standards.

Jan. 2008
"Wolves are removed from the federal endangered species list, giving states a blank check to slaughter the animals." (NRDC 2010) But at least if they are hunted down, they won't mate with humans and create werewolves, something I suspect Bush's weird science could easily imagine.

2008
"When considering protections for the polar bear under the Endangered Species Act, the Bush administration ignores the impact that oil and gas exploration off the coast of Alaska would have on polar bears." (NRDC 2010)

Maybe he already knew McCain would choose Palin?

Feb. 2008
"The U.S. Court of Appeals for the D.C. Circuit rules that the EPA illegally evaded safeguards requiring deep and timely reductions in toxic air pollution, including mercury, from coal-fired power plants." (NRDC 2010)

And then there are the thousands and thousands of pages of regulations Bush's hand-picked legislation-trashers wrote, all in aid of keeping their jobs, no doubt, and keeping to Bush's agenda that nothing mattered but bin Laden. Or was that Saddam Hussein? Or maybe nothing mattered but education. Or perhaps nothing mattered but removing regulations in this segment of life, as he was removing them in others.

Without Bush's activities, the BP disaster might well not have happened. It was his administration that opened the door to wildcatting in the worlds' oceans off the US as no one had done before. As a result, we were treated to a magnitude of disaster such as no one had seen before.

Greeder Wannabe Bush himself was arguably the single worst environmental disaster since 1864, when President Abraham Lincoln signed the act that gave the state of California a great area of natural beauty in Yosemite Valley, on the condition that they would "be held for public use, resort, and recreation... inalienable for all time."(National Park Service)

***

It seems time ended the day George W. Bush took office. At least for lots of wildlife and as yet uncounted humans who have been damaged or killed by his toxic presidency...and indeed, the entire Baby Boom which as been all but burnt at the stake by other generations blaming all of us for the execrable sins of one over-achieving dumbkopf.

CHAPTER SEVEN:
MAKING A NATION OF SERFS

Ronald Reagan's Tax Reform Act of 1986 (TRA) was a killer for the Baby Boom. It eliminated tax deductions for interest on consumer debt, making only mortgage interest deductible. The immediate effect of this was, naturally, for those burdened with consumer debt to attempt to remortgage their homes, or to acquire a second mortgage, or to sign up for the now-ubiquitous home equity line of credit (HEL).

So what?

The definition of a pauper is a person who owns not a single plot of ground to call his own. Although Boomers still held deeds to houses, they also had burdened those deeds so that their equity in the home — how much of it they really owned — was compromised. From the moment the first strapped homeowner rolled his or her credit card debt into an HEL, the financial freedom America stood for and all its much-heralded openness to anyone being able to prosper and even get rich went to HELl. At that moment, the nation became, to all intents, a nation of paupers.

From the point of view of the Greediest Generation, what could be better? The Boomers were much more likely to struggle harder to keep their home than they would to pay off their Mastercard bills; for many Boomers, their home was their only meaningful asset, and the one they had been drilled to believe would be unassailable as a foundation for their eventual retirement income despite its compromise by the TRA, a belief they unfortunately maintained until the George W. Bush financial disasters of 2008.

The 1950s really were the golden years, but not for us

All that would be bad enough, but apparently, it *wasn't* bad enough. A 2000 article by Robert M. Dunsky and James R. Follain, published in *Real Estate Economics*, noted that although mortgage and home equity loan interest was still nominally deductible, the changes in the tax code made it less likely that homeowners/consumers would rely on the tax advantages in order to invest in a home in the first place...if, indeed, they could somehow save enough money for a down-payment. (Dunsky and Follain 2000) To repeat: The definition of a pauper is a person who owns not a single plot of ground to call his own.

Judith Yates, in a 2007 white paper, profiles home ownership as an "aspiration of households in the 1950s and 1960s, as a driver of inequality for their Baby Boomer children in the 1970s and 1980s, and as a fading dream of their grandchildren from the 1990s to the present. It begins with the rise of home ownership in the immediate post-WWII period [when the Greediest were building families and personal wealth] and ends with the rise in rental investment that dominated the most recent house price boom [catching Boomers and Boomers' children in that net]. A key concern, identified in Chapter 1, is the decline in home ownership rates for younger households over the past 30 years."

Yates also noted that, "The economic certainty and stability associated with the steady economic growth, low unemployment and low inflation of the 1950s and 1960s was shattered by a slowdown in economic growth and the simultaneous onset of both high unemployment and high inflation. The latter created pressures on mortgage markets, which initially squeezed the amount of funds available for lending for housing, and ultimately contributed to the removal of the regulations that had kept housing interest rates relatively low." (Yates 2007)

That sounds *exactly* like America during those periods. But it wasn't; Yates was describing the Australian experience. Imagine how much worse it was in America, exacerbated by Reagan's TRA.

Dunsky and Follain explain how it operated in the United States under Reagan's income transfer to the banks and the wealthy:

> First, TRA increased the size of the standard deduction; and, second, it reduced the number of expenses that can be itemized. By themselves, these provisions increase the difficulty of a taxpayer filing as an itemizer (vs. taking the standard deduction) and reduce the tax savings associated with mortgage interest for some....These latter two provisions work to reduce the taxpayer's reliance upon home mortgage debt, because they reduce the tax savings associated it. Instead, these homeowners will find it more profitable to use more of its own assets (e.g. liquidate some stocks or bonds to pay off mortgage debt) to finance homeownership. These provisions also offset to some extent the positive impact on the demand for home mortgage debt associated with the non-deductibility of consumer interest. (Dunsky and Follain 2000)

In plain English, homeowners were not going to get the big mortgage interest deductions they had enjoyed up until TRA 1986. They would get no help in offsetting their initial investment or to handle ongoing upkeep expenses. They could take on more mortgage debt (second mortgages or home equity lines, in a sort of never-ending catch-up game), or they could do what Dunsky and Follain suggest they actually did in great part: liquidate some other assets — stocks and bonds, gold, inheritances if any (although the Greediest are notoriously stingy about that since they are, by self-proclamation, "out spending their children's inheritance") — to afford their housing. If they sold off those assets to pay current debt, they probably could not wait for favorable markets. But the wealthy, those still enjoying itemization on "business" second homes and donations and anything else the accountant could conjure, could certainly spring some cash to buy those assets at close to rock-bottom prices.

In fact, however, that's probably not what the wealthy did. According to a report by Moody's, the investment research company, wealthy people who experience a tax break don't spend the extra money, they save it. (Homan 2010) Although some of it will find its way into the economy via the circuitous route of investment by financial institutions, its effect is diluted. On the other hand, if they spent such windfalls, as less wealthy people generally do in their constant game of 'catch up' to obtain what they need, it would stoke the economy. In effect, by reducing the top marginal tax rate from 70% to 28%, Reagan all but ensured an economic slowdown. And an economic slowdown he got. Worse, that money has remained out of the market ever since, although a small bit of it might have returned as Bill Clinton raised the top marginal tax rate. Slightly.

As *Businessweek* reported on Sept. 14, 2010, "Tax cuts in 2001 and 2003 under President George W. Bush were followed by increases in the saving rate among the rich, according to data from Moody's Analytics Inc. When taxes were raised under Bill Clinton, the saving rate fell."(Homan 2010)

After Reagan put the skids under individuals and the economy as a whole, what was a homeowner to do? A few choices included taking on second jobs, or the non-working spouse could return to work, ensuring the continuing slide into household pain, anarchy and dysfunction. (This, too, would be of benefit to the Greediest; the second wave of the Baby Boom would be less inclined or able to have children, meaning less drain on government funding that the Greediest wanted for themselves. And, by ensuring a declining birth rate and/or children growing up damaged for want of traditional nurturing, the Greediest could be certain there would be no viable cohort to take care of the Boomers' needs when, and if, they retired.)

The rose-colored glasses of the Baby Boom

The TRA was far from being an improvement in the tax code for the middle class. Dunsky and Follain explain and lament that the tax changes caused weakening in a mortgage market expected to become quite lucrative to the mortgagors because of the tax change; had they a crystal ball, the Boomers caught in this trap would have been lamenting using their stocks and bonds to buy real estate that was going to tank just at the time they needed it, at retirement when it was supposed to have been the linchpin of retirement funding for many. Of course, we could not foresee Bush's depredations; we could not foresee Enron, WorldCom, AIG, BofA, subprime mortgages, Iraq, Afghanistan and so much more that made up the killer complex that finally made toast of the Baby Boom's present and future, and their children's and grandchildren's futures.

The government run by and for the Greediest had systematically forced the middle class into worse and worse financial positions. (The government is still run by the shadow Greediest, of course. Some functions, such as the Supreme Court, are still stacked with the Greediest who are continuing to carry out the program of making a nation of serfs who will do that master's bidding. Since the 2010 Supreme Court decision granting full personhood to corporations, the masters are likely to become the very companies already raping the Baby Boom and its progeny and pouring the money down the endless maw of unbridled greed re-opened by Ronald Reagan; that maw had been at least partially closed after the era of the robber barons, enabling the 20th century to be one of relative progress for the average citizen.)

Dunsky and Follain (2000) concluded, regarding the 1986 TRA, that "the elimination of interest on consumer credit as a deductible expense increases the cost of consumer credit relative to mortgage debt for households able to itemize expenses and encourages these households to place more reliance on mortgage debt and less on consumer debt." They had also noted that it was more difficult to itemize to realize the greatest tax advantage, as the TRA has also increased the standard deduction to a point that captured a goodly number of those who would itemize with a lower standard deduction.

Are all pigs are equal? Boomer pigs are less equal

Those consumers who fell into the category of those locked out of itemizing by the higher standard deduction still needed to make their lives affordable, however. With deductions for consumer credit interest a thing of the past, that left only mortgages and home equity loans, even if they were more expensive, in terms of offering deductions from the tax bill. In effect, the TRA:

- Forced consumers to diminish the value of their greatest asset — their home — by burdening it with mortgages, and,

- Forced them to spend a greater portion of their income in taxes because of the virtual elimination of any benefit from itemizing for a great number of taxpayers.

At last, all pigs were going to be equal: Equally ill-served by their government, and equally diminished in their quest for a sovereign plot of ground with a shelter all their own. Well, actually, some pigs were more equal than others. The Greediest were more equal; they had already realized great increases in the value of their homes, and keeping most of the money free of taxes via the capital gains exemption. And their incomes were such (and medical expenses beginning to be such) that itemizing did benefit them almost as much as it benefits the very rich.

On the other hand, the Boomers, in 1986, were at the peak of their earning years, establishing households if they could afford the downpayment (not likely for many with the flat wage increases and rise in housing prices) and educating children, while trying to prepare for their own retirement. Anything that increased their tax burden while diminishing the value of their greatest investment was obviously going to hit them harder than it would their parents who were, by then, selling off those homes at high prices to the Boomers who needed them, taking the cash and moving to retirement communities.

But the Greediest were not finished. In the two decades between the infamous TRA and the downward slide of the presidency of

Boomer embarrassment George W. Bush, the nation was in need of money, both to keep paying the COLA (cost of living adjustments) on current (Greeder) retirees, and to finance wars. Who would pay? Guess.

By the end of 2005, James R. Paterson, writing in the *ABA Journal*, noted that:

> Outstanding balances on credit cards have risen to more than $800 billion or $7,200 per U.S. household, and that doesn't include an additional $1.3 trillion in non-card debt for cars, appliances and personal loans. Moreover, a new bankruptcy law that takes effect this month will make it harder for consumers to get rid of their debt. It's easy to see why analysts and regulators fear that all of this could undermine the housing market, and mortgage lenders along with it.

Hmmmmm...

Remember, too, that this consumer debt was despite the non-deductibility of the interest, meaning much of it was rolled into a HEL. And remember, also, the flat wage picture for the working generation of the time, the Boomers.

The Greediest fix their one mistake

There was one fly in the Greeder retirement ointment: They were, between the flatlined wages and the TRA, running out of buyers who would qualify to buy their homes at inflated prices and let them run off to Sun City to play for 25 years or so until they went screaming to a nursing home, demanding gold-plated life support.

No problem.

The Greediest came up with a solution; the subprime mortgage. They had a lot of help — a lot — from Reagan's dismantling of the banking regulations. But they got some more from a fellow traveler from a generation tailor-made to help the older siblings they idolized (or at least, they do if Tom Brokaw, bard of the Greediest, is any indication): the tiny generation between the Greediest and the Boomers, often called the Silent Generation. Indeed. They silently went about their business of aiding and abetting the rape of the Baby Boom until Brokaw shot his mouth off. After Brokaw's sappy tome, they were emboldened to shoot their mouths off in public.

Worst American CEO, panderer to the Greediests' base instincts

Generally credited as godfather of the subprime industry, Angelo R. Mozilo was born in 1938. Mozilla, ranked by Conde Nast Portfolio as second on their list of "Worst American CEOs of All Time," was born in 1938. One of his chief protectors would have to be numbered Connecticut Senator Christopher Dodd who, like many VIPs, got immensely favorable mortgages from Mozilo's organization (and I use the term pointedly), Countrywide Bank, is also a member of the Silent generation, having been born in 1944. It's a shame that these two men, born on the cusp of a generation, sided with the one before. But they both stood to gain. Obviously.

All of a sudden, large numbers of lower income buyers were able to buy houses. If they were to fold their consumer debt into home equity lines of credit, when the inevitable realty slowdown arrived and prices dropped, it would also be inevitable that they would end up "upside down," that is, owing more for their house than it was worth, being unable to sell it, and having their mortgages foreclosed.

In many cases, it would have been inevitable even without the economic slowdown; illness, jobless and other ordinary stresses of modern American life would take a fair-size toll on these borrowers on the edge. Then, if they lost their house in foreclosure, there would be a further dampening factor for the housing market, depressing sales prices eventually.

The destruction of home resale prices was, of course, visited on the Boomers not just as the result of a normal "market correction," but directly because of the sub-prime greed run amok. The oldest of the Boomers were turning 62 just at the time of the housing crash and many wanted to sell out and retire. The avalanche of Reagan/Bush greed and Milton Friedman's unworkable monetarism connected, burying the dreams and often swamping the current realities of several generations of Americans beginning with the Boomers and proceeding henceforth.

The Greediest? By and large, they already had their profit and were well out of the resale housing market before the meltdown. Indeed, if they had the funds, it was a good time to scoop up some housing cheap and rent it out again to Boomers who had fallen on hard times. This would further damage resale prices for houses owned by Boomers. The downward spiral would be hard to miss, and hard to escape.

The fairytale continues; the nightmare lingers on and on and on...

The Greeder fairy tale/Boomer nightmare came true. A steep decline in the housing resale market damaged the ability of the Boomers to retire at all, never mind in the fine fashion the Greediest has been enjoying, based on increasing Boomer FICA payments to provide increasing entitlements...Social Security and Medicare...that the Greediest would all but murder to retain.

The convergence of the Bush juggernaut, the long-term effects of Reaganomics, and the intractable selfishness of the Greediest (who wrested a little more for themselves out of Medicare, while enriching the pharmaceutical companies and further impoverishing the still-working population), meant not only that Boomers wouldn't retire at anything like the age of retirement their parents enjoyed, or with half enough financing: It meant the generation that had been born into a global litter, scrambling for a workable teat from birth to retirement, would end its life as serfs.

How to solder the choke collar onto a serf

If you still doubt the malevolence of the Greediest and their anointed princes, consider this; Bush's bankruptcy law made suffering the American way of life, especially for Boomers and their children and their children's unfortunately clueless children. That latter is not meant as a jibe; it is meant as an indictment of two things, NCLB and the teabaggers.

Because of NCLB putting the cap on steadily eroding education in the US, the Boomers' grandchildren know no history, nor can they think logically. All they can do is take tests. Therefore, it is lost on them that it is not their grandparents who have caused societal upheaval; it is their great-grandparents, the Greediest, who have sucked the life out of their parents and grandparents for more than 40 years and will cease only when they cease to breathe.

The Teabaggers are equally culpable, and possibly more so; in an attempt at appearing younger and possibly brighter than they are, Baggers have consistently claimed to be Boomers when their given ages make them part of the Silent Generation or Greediest.

Since the generations after the Boomers, and particularly the current crop of NCLBed young people, know squat, the blame for the Greediest-Silent problems is pinned on the Boomers.

George W. Bush didn't really care if his own generation got blamed. George W. Bush is arguably the scourge of the Baby Boom generation, for this reason: Until George W. Bush, it was at least theoretically possible for those who had shifted their consumer debt to their home equity line (HEL), and had run up more consumer debt, to start over via bankruptcy.

George W. "Dubya" Bush is a Baby Boomer. But he's so much more, and so much less. The most worthless son of George H.W. Bush, and least competent member of a family best known for its dealings with Hitler's Germany until George H. W. entered American public service and then politics, Dubya was sacrificed to the cause. Too stupid to graduate from college without the family name to clear that path and excoriated by his professor at Yale as a dumbkopf, Dubya nonetheless presided over the most egregious dismantling of the American Constitution and American life imaginable. Actually, Dubya's destruction of the United States was *unimaginable*, and would have stayed so had he not been managed by characters who would have been deliciously evil as cartoons, but destructively evil in the flesh. (Their names, most prominently, are Cheney, Addington, Yoo, Gonzales, Rumsfeld, and Rice. Colin Powell had the good sense to get out before he was tainted too much. He had the good sense, and brains, to admit that he was embarrassed about being used by Cheney, albeit unwittingly, to sell the Iraq invasion to the United Nations.)

Their multifarious misdeeds of the Bush cabal — the Bush bankruptcy law, waterboarding, Abu Ghraib, Iraq itself, Afghanistan, Katrina, the financial meltdown, suspension of *habeas corpus*, stacking the once-Supreme Court, coat-tailing the likes of Sarah Palin, instituting No Child Left Behind etc. etc. etc. *ad infinitum* — were the death warrant for the American way of life in general and for the well-being of the Baby Boom generation in particular.

To recap: Why was the Baby Boom in particular damaged?

Because the Baby Boom generation had not yet stopped working and sold off assets to fund retirement. Nor did it have sufficient time to make up for the losses in housing value (the middle-class retirement linchpin, remember) and IRA/Keogh account losses during the debacle.

In short, the Baby Boom was eaten for lunch by the Greediest Generation, the Silent Generation, and a handful of younger wannabes such as, most prominently, George (Greeder) W. (Wannabe) Bush.

Ronald Reagan, the most deplorable excuse for a president the nation had ever known until the intractable idiocy of George W.

Bush, had set the table. George H.W. Bush prepared the menu (indeed, he and his buddies at the Bohemian Grove probably had it worked out long before Reagan got the White House gig). And Dubya, dressed in his variety of clever costumes depending on the event at hand, served up a tasty meal, complete with dessert....his bankruptcy act, the closest document in modern history to the once common and always exploitive articles of indenture.

The tastiest morsel of all: Every mother's son

The first bankruptcy act in the United States was the bankruptcy law of 1800. It was amended several times in the 1800s, and a few times in the 1900s. Each time, the specific terms under which bankruptcy could be declared were amended. But at no time — until 2005 when Bush and his allies at banks and credit card companies pushed through the oxymoronic Bankruptcy Abuse Prevention and Consumer Protection Act of 2005 (BAPCPA) — was the central concept of bankruptcy overturned. That central concept is the debtor's discharge and subsequent ability to make a fresh start.

The idea of a fresh start was unique when it was first implemented. Debtor's prisons were not effectively abandoned in the United States until 1833, and even now, failure to pay child support or purposefully violating the letter and spirit of the bankruptcy law can land a debtor behind bars.

But increasingly, throughout the 19th and 20th centuries, it was seen as ineffective to imprison debtors. In jail, not only would they not be able to repay their debts; they would cost the society money as well. Finding a means to help debtors to either repay their debts or discharge the debts so they could start anew (simultaneously spending money and keeping the hum of commerce going) seemed more advantageous to society. In U.S. bankruptcy law, two streams developed, the total discharge (usually referred to as Chapter 7, referring to the part of the U.S. bankruptcy code governing it) and repayment/reorganization plans (Chapter 13.) Most debtors chose Chapter 7; why prolong the agony? If one is going to get the black mark on one's record, just take it, get it over with, and move on.

Under the 1978 bankruptcy law (and virtually all previous laws), one could exempt one's home (with the cooperation of the lienholder) from liquidation to pay creditors as long as one could still make the payments. After the rise of the home equity line of credit (HEL), this was somewhat compromised; much consumer debt that would have been discharged without involving the family home had, after the Reagan Tax Reform Act, been incorporated into the mortgage or HEL, making it harder for consumers to pay the mortgage/HEL than it would have been in the days when consumer credit interest was deductible without being appended to the family housing debt.

In short, a person could be profligate with consumer debt, but not end up homeless under the pre-Reagan bankruptcy laws. They would be embarrassed, and rightfully unable to declare bankruptcy again for ten years, during which time anyone who granted credit would be necessarily be repaid, with interest. (If a debtor walked away from debt without declaring bankruptcy, there would be nothing to stop the creditor hounding the debtor forever, seeking judgments, attaching wages and so on. But he could not, ordinarily, be tossed into a jail cell.)

Is this just desserts? Yes and no. While it would be unethical to take on debt with no intent to repay, taking it on and intending to repay — but being subject to a negative event one could not foresee — is not unethical at all, despite the ignorant commentary in the press and especially on the Internet during the past two recessionary years.

Greed, not lending, is the devil

The fact is that money can be made by loaning funds to those who have a temporary lack of same; lenders build into their interest charges a certain amount to cover their expected losses on those who do not or cannot repay. In fact, credit has been a fact of life for thousands of years, and there's reason to believe human progress would have ground to a halt without it. It would have literally been impossible to erect great buildings or carry on great research without someone other than the builder and the scientist footing the bill. So, money was borrowed. Neither lender nor borrower is *a priori* unethical or stupid, as some of the commentary would have one believe.

Lending and borrowing are facts of human life; it is when either borrower or lender gets greedy that the system begins to crack. In the case of the sub-prime mortgages, the lenders were greedy, finding fiscally unsound ways to make unworthy borrowers appear creditworthy, at least until the Ponzi scheme developed a crack.

The government was greedy, too, or at least, politicians in government were as they knuckled under to the demands of the greedy consumer credit industry and allowed usurious rates while simultaneously closing the consumer escape hatch and exercising a panoply of income-deadening programs including allowing off-shoring, opening immigration quotas, and continuing the complete lack of worker protection legislation; worklife, in most areas, wasn't much better than it had been in 1900. Workers could be fired at will for no reason at all;

collective bargaining decreased steadily, especially after the Reagan years, and Dubya put the skids under such few protections from danger on the job American workers had ever enjoyed by tying OSHA's hands. (That's another entire book. But one need only look at the BP oil disaster in the Gulf of Mexico in 2010 to realize the extent to which the Bush administration failed to regulate much of anything; if one isn't going to regulate something as massive and dangerous as a deep-water oil rig, what hope is there for anything lesser? None.)

As a result, in the financial landscape since 1986, it has been irresponsible, not to mention unethical and downright cruel, to characterize most bankrupts as somehow flawed and unworthy. To chastise people pushed to the wall because of flat salaries (there was no real advance in salaries for the entirety of the Baby Boom's working life to date) for taking what little relief there was, loans and credit, is reprehensible. But the Greeder ethic has trickled down along with Reagan's economically disastrous programs and concepts, and too many holier-than-thou comments deride debtors without deriding the lenders who, absent stringent usury laws, unethically drained every last nickel out of the Baby Boom's piggy bank...and then stuck them into the pillories to boot.

Pillories. What other analogy is there for making a person whose finances have come to ultimate grief report to a court for decades, begging for some small measure of relief all the while being locked out of rebuilding with a clean slate, the emolument offered in all compassionate societies for more than 100 years? And being ridiculed and damned as well.

If you doubt that it was the intention of the Greediest to force every last nickel from their offspring and deny them any shred of solace or the ability to start anew, Brady C. Williamson, writing a well-researched answer, explains (please note the first date, a date when the Greediest were in power in the land):

> Since the 1960s, the consumer credit industry has crusaded for significant changes in the bankruptcy law to alter the balance between debtor rights and creditor rights, and the industry convinced Congress to change the Code to its advantage. In 2000, Congress adopted major changes in the law that would have made it more pro-creditor, *but President Bill Clinton exercised his veto.* (Emphasis added.)

> Creditors want a 'means test' that would eliminate the choice between Chapter 7 and Chapter 13. Creditors want consumers to be obliged to use Chapter 13 on the theory that at least some consumers could pay at least some of their debts. (2003)

And eventually, in the reign of King Dubya the Dumb, their wish was granted.

Note: Whenever the idea of a means test has arisen in regard to Social Security, the Greediest scream loud and long. If a person has sufficient personal income (dividends on stocks and bonds, family wealth, whatever) not to need this transfer of funds from current working people to current retirees, why should those retirees get a penny? Another interesting note: Social Security payments, unlike wage income, are protected under Dubya's bankruptcy law. Thus, The Greediest can rack up debt, take the dive, and continue to live much as they had before, only without the debt.

Recall that, under the 1978 law, it was possible to keep the family home if one could pay for it, and shedding other debt meant that some people could keep their home. One could also retain one's car, if one could pay for it, for traveling to work and such other mundane necessities, as long as the lienholder agreed. Not to mention the tools of one's trade: If you were a computer geek, you got to keep the equipment that allowed you to earn money. There were value limits under previous laws, but they were reasonably high and might actually have permitted bankrupts to successfully start over.

With Dubya the Dummy president, the creditors to whom Clinton had denied appeasement got everything they ever wanted. Under Dubya's 2005 law, it is almost impossible for a consumer to succeed at starting over after bankruptcy. They are almost forced into a continuing downward slide. The creditors? They are assured that no matter how unwisely they have lent money, they will be repaid. Nor was there anything in this Creditor Protection Act to ensure that creditors wouldn't raise interest rates high enough to force many millions more into bankruptcy who wouldn't have declared bankruptcy otherwise. Dubya helped the creditors to eat their cake and have it too…and the Boomer generation didn't even get crumbs.

Here's what Chapter 7 filers are allowed to keep under the Dubya's disastrous bankruptcy law:

- Their residence, up to $20,200 in value. No comment.
- Their car, up to $3,225. Very little comment.
- Their household goods and furnishings, clothing, appliances, books, pets or musical instruments up to $10,775, but no more than $525 per item. Warning: If

you've bought a pedigreed puppy, it might be seized by the court and sold to satisfy your debt. Lose the papers, and claim it's a mutt. Dishonest? Sure. But sometimes the only defense against the indefensible is a bit of civil disobedience. And next time, adopt a mutt from the shelter. Dubya's sheriffs won't get it, and you'll give another creature in need a helping hand, something Dubya wouldn't even comprehend.

- Tools of their trade, up to $2,025.
- The cash value of a life insurance policy, up to $10,775. This, too, is ludicrous. A whole-life policy is the only one likely to have any cash value before the insured's death. So, basically, Dubya is ensuring that if one attempted to build some retirement cash that way (many people do take out the cash value if they must), or to leave something for one's spouse or children, it won't happen. What does this say? Both you and your heirs and assigns will be tainted with the big red B, now and forever.
- Health aids. A boon to those already receiving Social Security retirement benefits...so, in 2005, no Boomers, only the Greediest and the Silents.
- Their right to receive Social Security, unemployment, welfare, veteran's benefits, disability, illness, alimony, support, crime victim's reparations.
- To the extent necessary for their support, the right to receive life insurance for someone who was supporting them or to recover damages for such a person's wrongful death.
- The right to recover damages, other than for pain and suffering, for personal injury, up to $20,200. (Harvard study 2005) Warning: Now is not the time to bring suit against the uninsured motorist who maimed you and win. Because even if you win, you won't win. Your creditor will.

Indeed, under the Bush bankruptcy law, the only ones who win are corporations and retirees from corporations, in short, the Friends of Bohemian Grove[19] and the Greediest.

---

[19] The Bohemian Grove, according to Wikipedia, is "is a 2,700-acre (1,100 ha) campground located at 20601 Bohemian Avenue, in Monte Rio, California, belonging to a private San Francisco-based men's art club known as the Bohemian Club. In mid-July each year, Bohemian Grove hosts a three-week encampment of some of the most powerful men in the world." Dwight Eisenhower and Ronald Reagan were members; George H.W. Bush and George Bush are members. According to the Sonoma County Free Press, "The membership list has included every Republican U.S. president (as well as some Democrats) since 1923, many cabinet officials, and director; & CEO's of large corporations, including major financial institutions." While Wikipedia is sometimes suspect, its information is based on reports dating back 30 years and to such reliable sources as the *New York Times.*

The Sonoma County Free Press (undated online entries) asks what isn't right about this. They answer: When powerful people work together, they become even more powerful. The Grove membership is wealthy, and becoming more so, while the middle class is steadily becoming poorer. This close-knit group determines whether prices rise or fall (by their control of the banking system, money supply, and markets), and they make money whichever way markets fluctuate. They determine what our rights are and which laws have effect, by appointing judges. They decide who our highest officials shall be by consensus among themselves, and then selling candidates to us via the media which they own. Important issues and facts are omitted from discussion in the press, or slanted to suit their goals, but they are discussed frankly at the Grove. Is there true democracy when so much power is concentrated in so few hands? Is there any real difference between the public and private sectors when cabinet members come from the boardrooms of large corporations? Is the spending of billions on weapons, which are by consensus no longer needed, really the will of the people? Or is it the will of General Electric, General Dynamics, and the other weapons contractors represented at the Grove?"

Could such a group be responsible for pushing the Baby Boom into serfdom? Who else?

Aside from relief, what else is lacking in Bush's law?

The word compassion is paramount in any discussion of bankruptcy today, unless we wish, as a society, to adopt the punitive approach of the Middle Ages. Today's bankruptcy law is devoid of compassion. It is punitive in the extreme for the modern world, and assumes that the beleaguered middle class is trying to pull a fast one by requiring credit counseling and forcing people into Chapter 13 filings. In fact, the United States General Accounting Office (Bowen 2010) has noted that in two-thirds of cases in which people are considering bankruptcy, the credit counseling session was ineffective — that is, the bankruptcy filing went forward. Still, it's a financial boon to credit counseling companies, and another way for the Greediest to maintain control of the Boomers.

Many bankrupts aren't slothful, they've been ill

Many of those households with no assets have already lost any they had, trying to pay for medical care. In fact, major illness accounted for half of US bankruptcies in 2001, derailing the right-wing claim that it is feckless ne'er-do-wells who clog the bankruptcy courts and run off with the nation's wealth.

The Harvard study (2005) reported that, "Illness and medical bills caused half of the 1,458,000 personal bankruptcies in 2001, according to a study published by the journal *Health Affairs*."

It would be difficult to think that the figure was not even higher now, after the decimation of the economy by Mr. Bush and friends, and the worsening nature of American health care. "Surprisingly, most of those bankrupted by illness had health insurance. More than three-quarters were insured at the start of the bankrupting illness. However, 38 percent had lost coverage at least temporarily by the time they filed for bankruptcy." (Harvard study 2005) They had also lost jobs, with 30 percent having a utility cut off and 61 percent going without needed medical care.

The same study noted that about 700,000 children were immediately affected by the 2001 bankruptcies, another figure that's doubtless higher now.

This research was developed by Harvard Law School and Harvard Medical School.

Correlation between lack of universal health care and bankruptcy

As of January 2010, the United States Congress was as far from enacting a meaningful national healthcare program as it ever was. Indeed, rather than electing a Democrat who at least had health care on her mind, Massachusetts voters elected to the seat held by the late Ted Kennedy, the nation's foremost champion of healthcare reform, a Republican who is adamantly opposed to healthcare reform. It is difficult to explain, especially as today's voters, unlike those filling the booths when Reagan was king, are Baby Boomers.

Perhaps they were just universally ignorant of the facts. So, here are a few for them to contemplate:

1. The Harvard report noted that today's health insurance policies offer little protection during serious illness. Insured people averaged more than $14,000 in bills for a serious illness; cancer patients ran up more than $35,000 in bills their insurance

didn't cover. And this doesn't even take into account the insurance company practice of recission, in which they look high and low for any reason, plausible or ludicrous, to deny those who are actually making claims for illnesses covered under their policies.

2. According to Dr. Quentin Young, national coordinator of Physicians for a National Health Program quoted in the Harvard study, "The paradox is that the costliest health system in the world performs so poorly. We waste one-third of every health care dollar on insurance bureaucracy and profits while two million people go bankrupt annually and we leave 45 million uninsured." (Lhotska 2005)

3. Dr. Young added that by spending what is now spend on private insurance with such disastrous results, we could have lifelong coverage for everyone and "end the cruelty of ruining families financially when they get sick."(Lhotska 2005)

That's peace-of-mind the Greediest Generation gave themselves, in the form of Medicare, just when they began to retire in the mid-1960s, but have consistently denied to their offspring. Why Boomers, now in at least nominal control of Congress, continue to deny it is mystifying, except for one thing: We drank the Kool-Aid. That is to say, we were educated to believe propaganda that served our parents, and we either accepted it in spades (think bank presidents), or rejected it completely (think aging hippies in tumbledown communes.) De facto Greeders in the form of bankers, or in the form of teabaggers or any other Alex Keaton-type of guy, won't vote for healthcare reform or its proponents citing bogus impediments to change; ageing hippies, having long since given up, probably don't vote at all. By splitting the Baby Boom generation so well (Vietnam was brilliant in that respect, and set the path for the Boomer generation forever), the Greediest guaranteed that they need not give up control until long after they are all dead.

Sometimes, small things mean the most

It was interesting that the legislation to force consumers to fold their consumer credit into their shelter costs happened when it did, several years after the Supreme Court made usurious interest rates — a prime factor in forcing consumers to shift their interest from non-deductible to deductible status, from credit card to HEL — not only possible, but highly lucrative to the domestic villains known as bankers.

In 1978, during President Jimmy Carter's tenure:

> The Supreme Court of the United States (SCOTUS), led by Warren Burger (as it was from 1969-1986) ruled in an obscure case about ambiguous wording in a small bank's lending documents. The ruling, probably as an unintended consequence, allowed states with liberal usury ceilings to export those rates to consumers in more restrictive states. In short, (and for example only) if North Dakota state law allowed lenders to charge 29 percent, and New York capped it at 15, then credit card issuers had an incentive to locate in North Dakota—or wherever they found the most liberal rates—and market their cards in New York, and everywhere else that had more stringent usury laws on the books. It was this ruling that allowed national marketing of credit cards, and also, because of the opportunity for lenders to charge high interest rates, to approve some less credit-worthy cardholders. (McBride 2009)

After that unsung (at least by the consumer press, shame on it) ruling, banks could cross state lines to rob consumers. Could smart citizens avoid getting credit in states that still had meaningful usury laws? Sure. But how long did it take for most states to lift their own usury limits? And how long did it take for banks in those states to realize that shifting their credit functions to a state that allowed higher interest rates was the thing to do?

Answer: A minute and a half, or not much longer.

To recap:

In 1978, the U.S. Supreme Court declares open season on consumers by ruling in an obscure case about lending documents.

In 1987, consumers lost the ability to let Uncle Sam help them with those usurious interest rates, when the interest deduction, on any loan except a mortgage or mortgage-linked instrument — was destroyed by Reagan's TRA.

But there was still bankruptcy, if the combination of usury, a flat wage table, and piling all debt into the mortgage payment was just too crushing, right? The 1978 bankruptcy law had affirmed the right to keep the house if one could afford the payments...a big if now that those payments included all the MasterCard charges rolled into the home equity line of credit. Still, it was something....

Oops. No it wasn't. The 1986 Reagan law eliminated that provision. What a shame, one might cluck, especially as it wasn't the usury or the compromised home ownership alone that forced those bankruptcies. Fifty percent of bankrupts cited major illness as part of the reason for bankruptcy. Two out of three cited job loss; it would pay to remember that, in an anti-union atmosphere — certainly the one that existed during the Reagan years — it was likely that anyone whose illness caused them to miss many workdays also might end up missing a job.

> *According to the Federal Reserve, fewer than nine percent of bankruptcies could be attributed to consumer fecklessness.*

Reagan was the harbinger of Doombya

In 2005, George W. Bush and his Congress of Fools mandated that any ordinary American who got into financial deep water due to any factor — job loss (many of which are attributable to Mr. Bush's policies), medical disaster (many of which are attributable to the longstanding and reprehensible lack of national healthcare in the richest nation on earth), or fecklessness — would be both a peasant and a slave. That is, that person would lose their home, and that person would have to beg the court for permission to eliminate *a portion* of their indebtedness, and would have to make payments to the court and report on progress to the court just as any criminal on probation.

The Bush bankruptcy law amounts—especially in the aftermath of his other predations—to no less than a roundup of American citizens to become donkeys imprisoned in misery by a morally bankrupt financial industry. (If you doubt the moral bankruptcy of American finance, you have avoided the news for the past several months.)

George W. Bush is either the greatest shill the world has ever known, making possible the Greediest's final feast on the carcase of the Baby Boom, or he is an amoral imbecile doing the best he can. Either way, the Baby Boom loses...and, because Bush is the age of the Baby Boomers, Baby Boomers are blamed by later generations for their own destruction. Brilliant, and doubtless worthy of the machinations of George *H.W.* Bush, the intelligent father of the Baby Boob; it wouldn't be surprising if the Bohemian Grove, of which George H.W. has long been a member, orchestrated it all.

In 2010, if a citizen wants to declare bankruptcy, he or she must pass a means test. Filers for a Chapter Seven bankruptcy must fall below median income for their state to file for complete discharge. If their income is more than that, and they can pay $100 a month toward their debt, they cannot get a complete discharge but must, instead, file a Chapter 13. Chapter 13 is just another word, under the new bankruptcy laws, for indentured servitude to the government.

Did I mention that, under the Bush bankruptcy law, those who owe taxes to said government cannot file at all until those taxes are paid? If they are broke, how is that supposed to happen? So they are locked into a no-win situation forever and ever.

> *While the pre-Dubya bankruptcy laws stayed evictions and foreclosures during the filing and discharge process, the new ones do not. No house, no car, no credit, no possibility of getting back to square one, never mind ahead.*

It's all much better, though, for those with more money. The more money they have, the more money they can keep. Bankruptcy laws? Oh, those are only for the little people. A report in the *New York Times* noted:

The wealthy can often stay millionaires because the laws in a handful of states—most notably Florida and Texas—set no limit on the value of a home that a bankrupt person can keep even as his debts are discharged by the court. So some people, as bankruptcy nears, sell their homes in states like New York and buy million-dollar homes, for cash, in Florida. (Norris 1999)

So here's the bottom line: To try to afford your house, your kids, their education and all that, you probably ran up some credit card debt. If you were ever late with a payment, your interest rate is hovering near 30% (And if you were fastidious in your financial dealings, it's still probably way over 20%.) Maybe you felt the best thing to do in that case, the responsible thing, was to roll it over into your home equity line of credit if you could.

Woe betide you if you did. Your house—if you lose your job, lose your insurance, get sick, have a child in college who is the hope of the future—is probably toast. Because you have tied your entire credit life to your mortgage, your house—your single asset of any value, your refuge from the government (well, it used to be before Bush's wiretapping and other potential incursions based on the weakening of habeas corpus and the extra powers the federal muscle crew got from the Patriot Act)—is tanked, one way or another. And you, my friend, are a serf.

Americans, 2010: Worse off than a medieval serf

No, you're worse than a serf. A medieval serf was granted his home as long as he worked three days a week for the lord of the manor and paid various fees the lord demanded. You're certainly not like a medieval freeman. In the Middle Ages, economies were expanding, and the work of freemen was paid for. Carpenters and suchlike needed to build infrastructure were particularly in demand. They could live anywhere they wanted. They could form guilds (unions) and do even better for themselves. (McBride, examiner.com, Jan. 30, 2009.)

Today, economies are shrinking, in the aftermath of the Bush debacle. And the same people who are usurping the nation's financing (insurance companies, banks, auto makers, et al) are also intent on preventing Boomers or their offspring joining unions.

Moreover, there was never any hope. Never. Not since at least the end of World War II, when the powers that be (corporations, the Bohemian Grove, counterparts worldwide) determined that the Middle Ages suited them very well. They would be the lords of the castle; they would appoint a few knights and sheriffs to keep the hoi polloi in line, and the rest would be made to settle for crumbs and be thankful for that.

CHAPTER EIGHT: REAGANOMICS TO THE BUSH MELTDOWN

Ronald Reagan made a handsome poster boy for the ignorance and/or cupidity with which the Greediest ran the nation when they were in positions of power in government and corporate America, not to mention education.[20] During his tenure, the distribution of the nation's wealth began a dramatic change. Between the 1940s and the early 1980s, the top ten percent of Americans took home 30 to 35 percent of the national income. Beginning during Reagan's term, the share of the top ten percent rose to its recent 45-50 percent level; recent research suggests it is now, one decade into a new millennium, much higher than that.

This information was developed by Prof. Emmanuel Saez of the University of California at Berkeley (website: http://elsa.berkeley.edu/~saez/), and recently reported by Richard Wolff, who also notes that the thirty years after World War II ended were, in contrast, relatively good for workers. That is, for the Greediest. (Wolff 2010) Note again: The Greediest' rise to the top was made possible by their parents' actions, including the GI Bill. As the Greediest began to fill in the top ranks as their parents retired, they completely ignored the generations after their own, establishing a credo of personal aggrandizement unmatched until the worst of the Baby Boom

---

[20] It was in school that the Boomers were beaten up with the evils of socialism. The evils of fascism? Not so much. Hence, Boomers like Rush Limbaugh vent their spleen on socialism, clearly the lesser of two evils if one is a worker and not living in a *bona fide* democracy, and behave like Nazis, clearly an evil for all concerned, except the few at the top making the rules.

— bankers, George Bush and suchlike — applied the lessons learned from their parents, the Greediest.

A word about Dick Cheney: He is *not* a Baby Boomer, and arguably, he and his unconscionable offspring Liz, whose flawed term paper formed the basis for Guantanamo detention and waterboarding, etc., were the architects of the rapid conglomeration of the threads in government, business and society that culminated in the Meltdown. Cheney is a member of the Silent Generation, Brokaw's generation…the generation that venerated the GI generation, donating a completely undeserved highest accolade, greatest, upon them.

The Bush Meltdown, while expressed as an implosion of banking and housing markets, would better be expressed as a plague, affecting the entire body politic, and caused by the infection of greed initiated by the generation that found that, unlike all previous human generations, it could ignore the future and take everything it could get its hands on, ultimately disappearing into black holes like Sun City, AZ, from which no benefit ever flowed back out.

Wolff attributes the worsening of income inequality to a combination of rising productivity and flat wages. The flat wages, as mentioned elsewhere, were caused partially by too many workers for the available jobs and a weakening of collective bargaining. The rise in productivity was helped by technology so employers didn't need to raise wages, Wolff says, to extract more production. Wolff notes, "Employers and those they support (share-holders, top managers, professionals, etc.) thus 'earned' ever more as workers' incomes stagnated. That top 10 percent got an ever bigger share of the total national income, while the other 90 per cent of us were left with an ever smaller share." (2010)

"Unions have declined for several mutually reinforcing reasons: deregulation, industrial change, globalization, and increased employer resistance (often abetted by lax government enforcement of the right to organize). As the union percent of the workforce declined, first slowly in the 1970s and then precipitously after 1980, so, too, did their ability to enforce the social contract and to bargain for the wages and benefits that rose with productivity. The union wage premium has diminished, and unions have had to fight defensive battles to slow the decline in health care and pension coverage, and to shift the costs and risk of these benefit plans form employers to workers." (Kochan 2007)

Wolff is too kind; he says that many Americans didn't know that they were falling behind because of changed social conditions; he claims the unwillingness of employers to pay higher wages when productivity increased was "just business."

Wrong. Because of the assault (ongoing) on collective bargaining and the opening of the immigration floodgates (creating the illusion that there were tons of workers for every job, qualified or not), employers saw an opportunity to grab all they could. To say that the Greediest were not good at sharing is an understatement. And then, like all good and selfish bullies, whenever they were pressed into sharing, they took their marbles and went home.

Wolff is right about much of it, though. Because American workers didn't know why their paychecks were flatlined when they were doing all they could and then some, they simply got depressed and suffered low self-esteem, he notes.

This, too, played into the Greediest's hands. The Boomer generation, recall, had had to claw and fight for every morsel of success in overcrowded classrooms. It had had to live cramped three to tiny dorm rooms meant for two when they got to college, unlike the relatively palatial conditions provided under the original GI Bill. Boomers were either drafted to serve in Vietnam, wangled a deferment (non-Boomer Dick Cheney had *five*) if they were teachers or still in school when the dreaded notice came, or refused to serve and were branded cowards and worse. Girls were not exempt; a girl was branded by the actions of the guy she dated or married. Despite being branded cowards, as noted in the Introduction, Boomers volunteered for service in Vietnam at twice the rate the Greediest had volunteered for service in WWII.

Explaining Boomer Republicans

A generational cohort squeezed by overcrowding and then killed in a useless, unpopular war or reviled from refusing to serve in it, additionally battered by inexplicably flat wages after doing what they were told to do — get an education to get ahead, or learn a good marketable skill — were hardly likely to have the energy to rebel. Finally, in frustration, many of them, as Wolff again accurately says, turned to scapegoating others for the inexplicably rotten deal the American dream had delivered for them: suddenly, immigrants, politicians, and bankers became targets of high-volume rage. Some of the portion of the Baby Boom that felt its earlier efforts had been in vain became willing dupes of the Republican Party, never EVER the party of the common citizen, not even when Abraham Lincoln was elected as a Republican. Lincoln's aim was to preserve the economically attractive union, not to free the slaves. Indeed, he capitulated concerning whether new territories joining the union could elect to have slaves: They could.

It is inconceivable that anyone who holds to the egalitarian ideals of the Founding Fathers (despite Washington and Jefferson owning slaves: they admitted it was wrong and both thought it would cease over time) could become a modern-day Republican in America. The leadership is either the plutocrats who would just as soon have virtual slaves, or their dupes. In short, it is the Koch brothers, or the Teabaggers. What, one might ask, happened to the participants in and admirers of the Summer of Love? Has Woodstock been forgotten? Or have the plutocrats succeeded, by taking a leaf from the book of the Greediest, in fragmenting the Baby Boom generation? If they have, it is tantamount to eating their young yet again.

The problem is, of course, that the portion of the Baby Boom that still embraces progressive ideals, having had its protest days when it was 18-21, now feels too old to effectively protest. The fire in belly is gone; all that remains is an ineradicable sadness that so much could go so wrong so quickly and leave them worse off than they were when they were standing in protest crowds during Nixon's reign of terror, a relatively mild one from that gormless bully boy compared to the damage wrought by the unholy triumvirate of Bush, Cheney and Rove. To say the progressive segment of the Baby Boom is demoralized is putting it mildly; taking the excessive suicide rates displayed by the aging Boomers, it would seem they are in despair to a great degree.

"Workers — not just their relative incomes — were victimized by the country's divisive economic development over the last 30 years," Wolff (2010) says. Yes, but....

But...it wasn't a faceless concept — "divisive economic development" — that's at fault; it is greed. And that greed was most eloquently and incessantly expressed by the GI Generation, the Greediest Generation. The Greediest. Aided and abetted by many of the Silent Generation, and by those of the Boomers who lost their compass and have followed their parents down the road to Hog Heaven.

***

Almost 30 years ago, while working on a book about Social Security, I noticed that the numbers were such that my generation was going to be the first to eat cat food, although that image was born just about 30 years ago, when the Greediest were retiring better off than any generation in history. That didn't prevent them from wanting more, and manipulating the media in their drive to get it by cackling incessantly about how the rest of us wanted them to eat cat food. They were saying this while consistently buying retirement life-care homes, voting down school bond issues, and demanding cost of living increases in Social Security, while the working class suffered anti-COLA wages.

The idea of old folks subsisting on cat food seemed to disappear over time, but in February, 2010, it returned. Various writers began calling President Barack Obama's Bipartisan National Commission on Fiscal Responsibility and Reform (to deal especially with Social Security among other things) by another name: The Cat Food Commission. Who was it that called it the Cat Food Commission? Same folks as last time; the Greediest, but this time, accompanied by the Teabaggers. The Teabaggers are roundly viewed as Boomers. They are not. They are the tail end of the Silent Generation, a generation that seems to want to be Boomers, but isn't. At least it would seem that way from the way the Baggers claim to be Boomers, despite giving ages that make them Silents, when they are interviewed carrying their ludicrous signs at protests.

***

Thirty years ago, when I found the statistics regarding the future of Social Security, I was actually looking for reasons it was so hard to get ahead. One could not blame it on computers and offshoring as much as Wolff does. Indeed, very few businesses were computerized when the slide began, during the Reagan administration. There must, I thought, be other causes.

In retrospect, it is clear that the Great Communicator, the Greediest' Choice — Ronald Reagan — was implicated in the issue of Boomer wage stagnation.

The GI Bill had laid a great foundation for Greeder prosperity. The war in Vietnam, the first OPEC oil crisis, and the emergence of serious Middle East terrorism during Jimmy Carter's presidency all helped set the stage for the final act of *Eating Their Young*. Still, during Reagan's "consolidation of gains" presidency, no one could have foreseen that the play would have an Epilogue, with the lead played by the most imbecilic son of Reagan's vice president, George H.W. Bush, himself a scion of a family of Nazi sympathizers and a Bohemian Grove member in good standing. That son is, of course, the least able of any president in history, and the man any wealthy family would be very happy NOT to have as the first son, George W. Bush.

Despite his claims about less government and less debt, Reagan left three unfortunate legacies. Privately held debt increased from 22.3 to 38.1 percent of GDP, with the deficit in his last budget remaining where it had been when he arrived, at about 2.9 percent of GDP. (Niskanan 2002)

He had also erected trade barriers, more than anyone since Hoover (and history bears out what a lovely effect that had on the U.S. economy). "The share of U.S. imports subject to some form of trade restraint increased from 12 percent in 1980 to 23 percent in 1988."(Niskanan 2002) Reagan himself is almost off the hook for this one. He talked free trade, but pressure from Congress and threatened industries (doubtless run by those who had never had to compete, the Greediest) forced the barriers into being.

Finally, Reagan's administration, in its inept (not to say malevolent) inattention to the S&L crisis added $125 billion or more to the national debt. (Niskanan 2002)

But not to worry: The Greediest and more than a few members of the Silent Generation were served well by all that. It's the Boomers and their kids who are paying for Reagan's never-ending swan song.

Savings and Loss Crisis

Reagan's S&L crisis was another Greediest gift that keeps on giving, and one that allowed his vice president's family back into the fold of ultimate oligarchs. The Bush family ably helped continue the drain begun by Reagan. Indeed, Neil Bush was involved in the S&L crisis, and, while not criminally prosecuted, was sued and had to repay $50,000, a pittance next to the $1.3 million the failure of Silverado Savings & Loan, a Bush baby, cost the taxpayers.

A decade later, as the Bush family connived to shoehorn idiot son Dubya into the White House, Neil founded a company that would take full and expensive advantage of the US taxpayer under Dubya's No Child Left Behind educational debacle.

In 1999, with $23 million in investment from Daddy Bush and a host of international power brokers including a Russian billionaire on the lamb for various funny money dealings (how did Russia get any billionaires so quickly? Don't ask), Neil set up Ignite! Learning, which was in the money once it had sold its products to 13 school districts that used federal money to buy the workstations at $3,800 apiece. Neil Bush's salary was reported to be $180,000 a year.

What did Daddy Bush teach Neil about S&Ls as a good gamble?

As long ago as 1990, the *Washington Monthly* told us who had driven the Baby Boom into poverty, relative to the Greediest if not to the rest of the known universe. It was Ward Cleaver. (Bennet 1990, 38+) Cleaver was the father on the popular TV sitcom, *Leave it to Beaver*, and typical of the lower rung of the Masters of the Universe at the time. A white-collar flunky, Cleaver was undeniably the product of the GI Bill. He had a good job, and his wifey stayed home and raised two children in a sizeable house in a growing small city. There was never any suggestion that wifey actually did anything. She didn't volunteer at an animal shelter, and in light of the full skirts, perfect coiffure and pearls, she probably didn't scrub toilets, either. It's easy to assume she might have had household help; almost certainly, she had her bridge club and her hair appointments and the odd request to bake cookies for Beaver's class at school. (These would come out of a box from Duncan

Hines, no doubt, but be mixed up and baked at home to avoid "store bought" so she could be a real Mom.)

It was during the end of the period, the 1960s, that the scene began to be set for the Boomers to end up carrying the load, but getting none of the benefits. There was a hint of the changes in store for America.

Are the bulk of the Greediest guilty of eating their young?

First, it is wise to recall who was in charge of Congress and major corporations during the late 1950s, 1960s and 1970s. The Greediest. So, they had everything to gain by monkeying with banking regulations in ways that would serve themselves, and hang their offspring. While Ward Cleaver probably personally had no hand in the maneuvering, he did doubtless elect those who not only understood what was about to happen, but engineered it.

To begin: When the Greeder middle class shopped for a house in which the little woman would raise the two children, they had saved up a deposit, probably at a Savings & Loan (S&L). They trusted the S&L to keep their money safe. The Federal Deposit Insurance Corporation had, since 1934, guaranteed deposits up to $100,000. A middle-class house, in the mid-1950s, probably cost no more than $8,000, and the head of the household would have asked the bank for a loan for most of that.

He might have dealt exclusively with an S&L, and not with a commercial bank. They made their money, back then, by holding deposits and paying less interest on those deposits than on the money they loaned, supposedly made up of the bank's deposits.

Enter Fannie Mae and Freddie Mac...but not quite yet.

Back then, but not now, all sorts of regulations were applied to S&Ls, most of them removed either before Reagan took office, or during his term. It was because of the cutback in regulations that, all of a sudden (and just when the Greediest had achieved success and had money to spend or use to make more money), the regulations were substantially destroyed. S&Ls could suddenly back all sorts of things they couldn't have before. Low mortgage rates were one result; S&Ls could make up the money in other ways, now that they had been admitted as full players to the banking game.

Are you a Boomer or a Greeder?

S&Ls backed absurdly dumb construction projects; the rise of the S&Ls toward crisis was responsible for much of the DC beltway building overload. S&Ls offered ridiculously high interest on deposits; they had to. Their Ponzi scheme of attracting more deposits so they could engage in more stinky maneuvers depended upon it. In his lengthy 1990 article in the *Washington Monthly*, editor James Bennet wrote, "The vanguard of the Baby Boom and its elders (today's Americans over 40) made a fortune thanks to the thrifts' suicide subsidy. It stands to reason that, as the bills come due over the next 30 years, those wealthy people — not all taxpayers — should pay."(1990, 38+)

Bennet is right to an extent, but only the very first, very smallest portion of the Baby Boom would have been, by then, in a position to engage in this travesty. As has been outlined in the rest of this book, Baby Boomers have consistently had less money than their parents did at similar stages in their lives. It is likely that the number of Boomers who profited this way is exceedingly small.

Here's Bennet's test to see if you are an S&L greed participant or one of its victims:

Did you:

- Take out a mortgage in the fifties, sixties, or seventies?

- Invest in a money market fund in the seventies or early eighties?

- Buy a certificate of deposit in the past 10 years? (Meaning between 1980 and 1990.)

According to Bennet (1990, 38+):

> If you answered 'yes' to any of the above, YOU MAY HAVE ALREADY WON SEVERAL THOUSAND DOLLARS! You're at least a cause of the S&L crisis, if not a winner in the Bankers' Bailout Sweepstakes. In fact, aside from the not-insignificant question of intent, the main difference between you and the S&L crooks is that, collectively, you took a lot more money than they did. Oh, also: You've gotten clean away.

Very few Boomers can answer yes to those three questions, or even any two of them. Nonetheless, their children and grandchildren will be paying the bill.

The ever-popular theme from Shaft especially for Boomers

Paying the bill might not have been so bad if Boomers, like most middle-class Cleaver-type families they grew up in, had a mortgage for their house at 5.5%. But, in 1966, Congress decided S&Ls would be allowed to pay no more than 4 percent interest on savings, which meant they would have to double that on loans to make back enough money for solvency and perhaps profit. Plus, since all of a sudden, inflation was a factor in the marketplace, it meant they could keep making money on the loans they had made to the middle class homeowners five or ten years before.

The Federal Reserve was slow in adjusting the rates S&Ls could pay and charge at least three times between the late sixties and early eighties, Bennet notes. Depositors lost money by saving it when the interest rate fell below the inflation rate. Of course, that didn't stop the Greediest from recommending that their offspring save more money.

Bennet also notes that the federal government tried to support S&Ls' deposit rates by making it very difficult for small investors to make money any other way. Commercial banks were limited to paying lower interest on deposits than the S&Ls could pay. In 1970, "Congress raised the minimum investment in the more lucrative Treasury bills from $1,000 to $10,000 (at the time, the average thrift account was $3,045)."(Bennet 1990, 38+)

Here is the single statement that says it all:

> Now, if you'd taken out a mortgage in the fifties and sixties, you were a) at least in your thirties by the 1970s;

and b) a homeowner, i.e., probably on your way to being well off. "There's the unconscionable wealth transfer,' says Bert Ely. 'It's an intergenerational transfer. The young got screwed by the old'. (Bennet 1990, 38+)

About the Baby Boom: The oldest among them was 24 in 1970, probably still paying off college loans or trying to find a decent job. That held true for the Baby Boom even at 30; the generation is castigated for doing things...such as having children and buying houses...later than the Greediest. But they were otherwise engaged. It's not that they were saving themselves for more important work, as former Silent Generation Vice President Dick Cheney once infamously noted of his endless deferments of service in Vietnam.

Some Boomers were, instead, trying to survive pongee sticks, bullets and machetes in an Asian jungle. That delayed career- and family-starting, as did college and then grad school. People racked up graduate degrees at an almost alarming rate (meaning there would be no college teaching jobs for them at the end of the quest) because one could get grants and loans when one couldn't get a job. In addition, looking for a decent job in a market diluted by the sudden flinging open of the immigration doors the Greediest had kept firmly shut while they were starting out was another way the Boomers were kept out of the American dream, all the while being told that they were selfish by the very Greediest who were in charge of who got the goodies and who got the shaft.

Trail of tears traces the mortgage screwing of the Baby Boom

In 1967, a nice home with three bedrooms and two baths cost about $30,000, depending on locale. Mortgage rates were at 6 percent. By 1976, a similar home carried an interest rate of 8.5 percent.

But don't feel sorry for those who waited until 1976 to buy; inflation was making that interest rate seem like a bargain, and, besides, home values were going only in one direction, up. In addition, half of the interest on the mortgages was deductible.

In fact, with inflation driving wages up even if ever so slightly, those who had gotten into mortgages before 1976 had money to burn; those who hadn't were, of course, paying ever steeper rents on their apartments as landlords took advantage of the inflation rate to widen the spread between their own mortgages and their rental income. ("I have to raise the rent to match inflation," the landlords explained, failing to add that their own mortgage was fixed at a much lower rate than inflation. For the landlords, who were certainly not Boomers, it was all profit. Easy unearned profit, a Greediest hallmark.)

In addition, of course, the rent-gouging made it likely that the Boomers caught outside the mortgage market would have an ever more difficult time coming up with down-payment money, unless their own pay increases outstripped the inflation rate. As noted earlier, this was not likely because:

> a) There were too many Boomers looking for too few jobs,
> b) The immigration doors had opened letting lots of workers into both the low-level and highly technical jobs, and,
> c) Many Boomers were earning advanced degrees, making them less employable, not more, in a glutted market.

It bears repeating: In 1976, when the way was opened for the Greediest and the Silent Generation to cash out at Boomers' expense, the oldest Boomers were just turning 30. That would be a reasonable age in most generations to assume a great number of the cohort was ready for home ownership. For the Boomers, however, with the Vietnam delay, the no-jobs/advanced degree delay, the new possibility of putting off starting families via reliable birth control and the immigration pressure, thirty-year-olds were just barely at a stage to buy houses, and the 30-year-olds were by no means the largest part of the Baby Boom. The bulge came several years later; in 1976, people in their early and mid-twenties were not generally candidates for home-buying.

Use money to make money. No money? No money.

By now, one cannot help but note that the Greediest cohort had money to burn. What to do?

They couldn't put it in S&Ls where every dollar saved was a dollar lost, considering the interest paid and the galloping inflation. And then, suddenly, money market funds crawled out of the banking basement and into the front window.

Money market funds have been around since the early 1970s. The funds pooled shareholders' cash to make loans at the prime rate. Through their banks, consumers could get in on the action for a measly $1000 a pop. The return was much greater than S&L or bank ordinary interest. No wonder assets in money markets grew from $3.9 billion in 1977 to $208 billion in 1982. (Bennet 1990, 38+)

Of course, the Greediest shifting their money from S&Ls to money markets at commercial banks meant the S&Ls suffered.

Naturally, the S&Ls went to the federal government for a bailout. (And you thought the Bush meltdown was a first!) But they didn't do that before they made disastrous loans trying to cover their money market commitments with decreasing deposits elsewhere, and with all those low fixed-rate mortgages on the books. In 1981, 85 percent of S&Ls lost money (Bennet 1990, 38+), despite Congress allowing them, that same year, to offer adjustable rate mortgages to compete with commercial banks.

It was not enough to save the S&Ls. At today's rates, the bailout we paid for our parents' prosperity is about $147 billion. In 1981, the Greediest were beginning to retire, so many of them got out of the increased tax burden to pay for the bailout. But the Boomers didn't.

All of which meant Boomers had even less money to save and take advantage of the money markets. That's too bad, because "between 1979 and1981, interest income for individuals and institutions shot up 42 percent, until it accounted for 13 percent of all personal income. Since that average included tens of millions of people who had no interest income at all [primarily Boomers], chances are that our friends have been doing quite well for themselves." (Bennet 1990, 38+)

Needless to say, Boomers had even less chance of saving enough for a downpayment on a house.

What if a rescued S&L still bottomed out? No problem for the Greediest; all they had to do was make sure all their accounts were under $100,000, so they'd be fully insured, although it would be troublesome to have to fill out paperwork to get the money...and just think of the interest they would lose! Still, it would be "One minor inconvenience for a *Money* reader, one giant disaster for American taxpayers." (Bennet 1990, 38+)

Money tells what makes the world go around

Who were the *Money* readers? The Greediest, of course, in droves. *Money* readers were 131 times more likely to have a brokerage account than the average American. They were 79 percent more likely to own securities worth more than ten grand and they were also "exceptionally acquisitive." What? How can that be? The media has been full for two decades of stories about the Boomers being the Me Generation. And now we find out that the Me Generation was the Greediest all the time!

> *The Me Generation? Think it's the Boomers? Think again. It's the Greediest. The GI Generation, elevated to a pinnacle of marketing power for itself by Tom Brokaw's addlepated tome.*

It's not really that surprising. It's called projection: The Greediest projected their own selfish attitudes onto their offspring. So perhaps we can put to rest that tired concept for all time. The Boomers are not the Me Generation; that title properly belongs to the Greediest. If Tom Brokaw's "Greatest" Generation is great in anything, it is great in this: Stealth. It hid its complicity in the military industrial complex. It hid its complicity in the Reagan-era monetary depredations. It hid its acquisitiveness even from its own children, who — while suffering the flatest wage picture in a hundred years — were "guilted" into providing COLAs and god-knows-what so the Greatest Greeders the World has ever known could retire to Sun City, and shift the blame for every blasted negative factor in society directly onto the shoulders of their own children, the Baby Boom.

Service journalism for the Greed Generation

Money served its readers well. It advised them to keep less than $95K in their S&L accounts so that they wouldn't lose interest already earned if they had to seek the $100K guarantee.

By 1984, only the Greediest and the very oldest Boomers (if they had been lucky in other way, such as no student loans, no Vietnam service, etc., and an early start to their careers) had more than "three times the net worth of heads of households who were younger than 35...."(Bennet 1990, 38+) They also had "had more than twice as much money in CDs and other interest-earning deposits as those under 35; almost three times as much in investments like money market funds and bonds; almost twice as much in stocks and mutual funds; and almost twice as much in home equity." (Bennet 1990, 38+)

Home ownership had risen steadily since 1940. It even continued to rise during the first few years of the Boomers' first cohorts adulthood; it would have had to, even at low percentages of Boomer buyers because of the enormous numbers of potential home-buyers involved, plus the newly opened immigration flood gates.

In 1980, when the Boomer cohort was beginning to enter their peak earning years, home ownership began to decline.

Bennet wrote:

> In *The Politics of Rich and Poor*, Kevin Phillips writes, 'In 1980, 23.1 percent of people under 25 owned their own homes. By 1987 that rate was down to 16.1 percent.

Among those between 25 and 29 the rate fell from 43.3
percent to 35.9 percent. . . . To more and more citizens,
the American dream of homeownership was becoming
just that — a dream.' Those young Americans are too
busy covering their elders' mortgages to afford their
own. (1990, 38+)

In short, the Baby Boom generation was well on the way to
being a generation of landless peasants. What is the definition of
a serf? Again: A serf is a landless peasant.

The Greediest, and their avaricious leaders from Ronald Reagan
to George W. Bush, didn't really need the meltdown Bush's
handlers engineered to acquire the serfs they wanted; they'd
been working at it, quite successfully, for half a century. By
2008, it was a virtual fact even without stripping the Baby Boom
of the last remnants of its future.

CHAPTER NINE:
RETIREMENT, OR, FOR BOOMERS, WHAT RETIREMENT?

What retirement indeed? In mid-2009, early Baby Boomers were still facing a life without retirement; middle Boomers might or might not make up the losses their 401(k)s had experienced in 2008. Late Boomers stood a better chance. But retirement as our fathers and mothers know it? Very, very unlikely.

First, Social Security is, in case you've been living on another planet for a couple of decades, perennially "in trouble," but at no time more than now and in the near-term future.

Second, retirement benefits once provided by employers are about as scarce as a Republican with a sense of compassion, and for about the same reasons. Just as Reagan, with his numbskull trickle-down theories, was ascending to the national stage, Congress decided to award U.S. corporations more profit by pushing the onus for retirement funding onto the employee. One might call it a strict constructionist view of creating self-reliance. Or one might more aptly call it what it was; another attempt by the Greediest to transfer the next generation's money to their own pockets via the stock market in which they were invested and which would return greater dividends after the release of corporate income from providing for the people who made the company — whatever company — what it was. Clever. Especially as they were already vested, and thereby assured of their company-sponsored retirements.

Social Security, as mentioned, has been perennially saddled with the spectre of future shortfalls. That helped, of course, to encourage Congress to raise the age for receiving Social Security while paring the benefits.

The missing COLA

They missed one place to cut, though, until the financial debacle of 2008; they had enacted automatic cost-of-living increases, but there was no increase in cost of living in 2008. Therefore, the Greediest receiving benefits missed out on that little bit of something for nothing. And the weeping and moaning about it was deafening. Indeed, it is very likely that one glitch in the Greediests' march toward bigger and better retirements through plunder brought on the Teabaggers. And, as noted earlier in this book, the Teabaggers who claimed to be Baby Boomers were too old to be Baby Boomers, and either lamented that lack, or wanted to make sure future generations blamed the Baby Boom for the problem.

The fact is, every working person since Franklin D. Roosevelt's administration pushed the Social Security legislation through Congress (in the depths of a Depression!) has been able to retire better, on average, than those who came before. The Baby Boom is the first generation whose retirement is in serious jeopardy, and who will retire infinitely worse off than their fathers and most of their grandfathers did.

Retirement becomes source of double taxation for Boomers

For almost the entire Greediest generation, Social Security benefits were not taxed. Not so anymore. Today, if a worker "earns more than $25,000 and files a single return, or if a married couple earns more than $32,000 and files a joint return, up to 85 percent of the Social Security benefits are subject to federal income tax."(Friedman 2009)

It is, at the very least, double taxation. Workers already paid income taxes on what they paid in FICA (Federal Insurance Contribution Act). Note: FICA is *not* a contribution. It is mandatory. Calling it a contribution is another example of the government's continual ploy to make Americans think they have choices when they do not.

In the post-Bush Meltdown business environment, older Boomers are being forced to take their Social Security early just to live; their unemployment has run out and they cannot find jobs. "In August, the average time unemployed for those 55 and older was slightly more than 39 weeks, according to the Labor Department, the longest of any age group. That is much worse than in August 1983, also after a deep recession, when someone unemployed in that age group spent an average of 27.5 weeks finding work." (Rich 2010) Note: in 1983, it was the Greediest and Silents who were affected, but even so, not nearly as badly affected as the current retiring generation, the Boomers.

In 2008, the first year of the Boomer generation was able to take early benefits, at age 62. "Taking Social Security at 62 means a retiree would receive a 25 percent lower monthly payout than if she worked until 66." (Rich 2010)

By 2011, that group will reach age 65 and be entitled to full benefits. Some will have taken benefits early, but at that point, virtually the entire first year of Baby Boomers will be receiving their Social Security and Medicare benefits. By the time the last Boomer in the last year of the Boom generation retires and takes benefits, the total number of beneficiaries will be 77 or 78 million. Result? "This will create a financial train wreck for Social Security, Medicare and Medicaid and all other programs for the elderly," according to John C. Goodman, president of the National Center for Policy Analysis (2010).

Bush's Fat Cat tax cut puts skids under Boomer retirement

Social Security cash flow problems are not waiting for the retirement of 77 million Baby Boomers. It has already started. For many decades, both Social Security and Medicare took in more in payroll taxes (FICA) than they spent. However, in 2003 and 2004, for the first time, the programs took in less than they were committed to pay out, requiring a subsidy of about $45 billion from general funds.

This should not be terribly surprising: the Bush administration cut taxes for the wealthy, who would be paying into Social Security at the top of the scale (even though the percentage they paid is far less than the percentage the lowest earners paid from their salaries.) Their top-of-scale payments would have gone a long way to balancing the preponderance of bottom-of-scale payments by Boomers, who had experienced flat wages their whole working lives relative to inflation, and younger workers at the beginning of their wage-earning years.

Making matters worse, the Bush regime covered its working- and middle-class impoverishment tricks with a couple of clever dollar giveaways that could be spent to ramp up the war-ravaged domestic economy so that, a) Halliburton, Blackwater, et al could continue to rape and pillage via domestic investment, and, b) the population, always gullible, would think it had gotten something for nothing when the fact is, they got nothing for something. They got virtually nothing in return for financing two illicit wars and other Bush entertainments, such as the bankruptcy reform of 2005 that basically made Americans into serfs owned by financial and credit card companies, and, in 2006, the Pension Protection Act.

Correction: They got less than nothing. They got the kick in the teeth that is the hallmark of imbecilic bully boys like Bush and Rove, and doubtless the entertainment for ethics-absent mephistophelian predators like Cheney.

Ministry of Truth strikes again, with pension protection — Not

The Pension Protection Act forced employers who offered the old-fashioned and very worker-friendly defined benefit plans to increase premiums paid to the Pension Benefit Guaranty Corporation, a program that protects the pensions of "44.1 million American workers and retirees."(Friedman 2006)

In 2006, it is safe to say, virtually no Boomers were among the retirees being protected; virtually all recipients of these now almost-extinct plans were members of the small generation before the Boomers, the Silent Generation, or the Greediest themselves. It is also safe to say that the employers didn't take the increased "donations" from their own pockets; they couldn't take them from the pockets of those receiving the pensions. Who does that leave? Right. Current workers, the vast majority of whom, in companies stable enough and old enough to have such plans, must be assumed to be Boomers.

It must be mentioned that there is no federal program comparable to the Greeder-friendly Pension Protection Act to protect Boomer money in IRAs and 401(k)s. In fact, those instruments lost enormous amounts of value during the Bush financial meltdown of 2008. There is no way for Boomers nearing retirement to recoup their losses in time; there is no federal agency waiting to make up the difference, as does the Pension Benefit Guaranty Program for defined-benefit pension plans that experience loss for one reason or another. (Well, sort of. In fact, the Pension Benefit Guaranty Program is another boon to corporations and beastly useless, most of the time, to employees.)

The dearth of FICA contributions will continue

Baby Boomers are entering their retirement years in their usual enormous numbers. For the first time in history, even before their retirement and while all that great band of them was paying into their parents' Social Security and Medicare, those two programs had a $45 billion shortfall.

Here's Goodman's most alarming conclusion for Baby Boomers:

> Without changes in worker payroll tax rates or senior citizen benefits, the shortfall in Social Security and Medicare revenues compared to promised benefits will top more than $2 trillion in 2030, $4 trillion in 2040 and $7 trillion in 2050! (2010)

Is it likely payroll tax rates will rise? Considering that young people are entering the workforce later than ever before and are moreover entering it at lower pay levels, what can one conclude? Nor is late employment start and lower pay the entire story.

According to Meridith Levinson (2009):

25- to 34-year-olds make up the largest group of underemployed workers. More than 2 million 25- to 34-year-olds are working part-time jobs because they can't find full-time jobs or because their hours have been cut—which is more than any other age group.

That all signals that it will be difficult, if not impossible, for the government to corral enough extra income — even absent the bank and automaker bailouts of 2008 and 2009 and the lowest tax quarter of all time in early 2009—to make up shortfalls.

There is only one conclusion: Baby Boomers will pay more of their own way in retirement than their parents or the small generation before them ever dreamed of doing. Considering their flat wages, the parental drains against their income, the fact of massive job loss in their age group after the 2008 meltdown, what, exactly, are the Boomers supposed to use for this?

In 2010, a fifth of the out-of-work people in Seattle were over age 55 and claiming extended benefits because they had been out of work so long. (Rich 2010)

Since the Nixon/Ford era, the companies that employ Boomers have had the option of the defined contribution plan, under ERISA, the Employment Retirement Income Security Act. Like the names of government departments in Orwell's 1984, the name of this act is precisely the opposite of what it appears to intend. It is a veritable "Ministry of Truth" for retiring Boomers, if indeed such a creature is to be found.

ERISA and the IRA, or how to ensure the largest-ever generation dies the most broke

Until 1974, companies offering pensions, and they were many, offered defined benefit plans. In short, a secretary knew what she could expect to retire on by figuring her likely Social Security income and her pension. The same was nominally true across industry, as people from secretaries to CEOs had defined benefit plans and Social Security, plus whatever they could save, or in the case of CEOs and executive personnel, whatever they could demand from the board of directors.

Defined benefit v. defined contribution pension plans

ERISA changed all that, conveniently just in time for the Baby Boom to begin assuming real jobs, not part-time college employment, and preparing for their own eventual retirement.

Today, only the top rung of the top rung has benefitted from ERISA. As Jane White (2010) puts it:

> Here's the raw deal in a nutshell: Unless you've got Chief and Executive in your job title — including "Ousted Disgraced CEO" — you are probably pension-poor, even if you earn a six-figure salary. That's because only 11% of the private sector population is covered by a regular pension. Unlike during the postwar Fabulous Fifties and the Soaring Sixties when America was a "fortress economy" and almost half of the private sector was covered, currently even most employees of big companies can't count on one. Only 17 of the Fortune 100 companies offer a traditional pension to new hires.

There are a few essential words and phrases here that should signal to Boomers that, as usual, their elders are giving them the shaft. "Fabulous Fifties and Soaring Sixties" is one. "New hires" is another. In short, if you began with one of those few companies in the 1950s or 1960s, you are covered. If you joined in the 1970s, 1980s or especially the 1990s (got all the Boomers in the mix now), not so much. The Greediest are basically covered, and maybe some Silent Generation members. But Boomers? You know the answer.

Forcing workers to turn over their retirement to someone else

ERISA allowed employers to switch from defined benefit plans to defined contribution plans. No longer could one calculate what one might have to live on in retirement; one could, however, easily calculate how much money was being shifted out of current paychecks, and, if one were particularly money savvy, one would understand that the money was at risk in a volatile stock market, and that there was no one accountable for what might happen to that money. No safety net. No government body equal to the Federal Deposit Insurance Corporation (FDIC) to cover at least a portion of any losses caused by company failure.

Not only that, but the funds contributed to IRAs and Keoghs were at risk to the employee, but not under the employee's control. What? You're being told "trust me" by financial organizations and have no option to oversee what they're doing? Yup. Who would *DO* that? Those with no other options because, a) the companies had been allowed by law to use their worklives up without providing cent one for their after-work lives, and, b) they already had a sinking feeling that Social Security would not be around for them.

Invitation to a dance of death

When the Greeder government set up the IRA and Keogh program rules in 1975 (self-funded investments for the self-employed and those employed by companies that didn't offer retirement plans), they declared that individuals could not direct their own tax-deferred retirement funds. By law, those funds had to be administered by someone else, meaning it was not as simple as the investor picking up the phone and placing buy or sell orders to his or her own perceived benefit; a fund had to be contacted, often paperwork needed to be filled in, and the amount of money one received on a sell order would reflect the time the fund got around to it, not the time the investor chose. The Greediest had set up a win-win situation for themselves, and for the financial companies they set up.

Financial companies leaped onto the Boomer Gravy Train, "managing" the investments for the few highly pressured Boomers who money but no time, what with the continued strain of competition to stay in place, to pore over the financial pages as so many of their fathers had done and to learn about investing. Indeed, because a worker could not manage an IRA or a Keogh, but was forced to turn it over to an outside party to gain the tax benefits, one might easily regard ERISA not as the Accountants and Lawyers Full Employment Act, as it was once laughingly known, but the Wall Street Robber Barons Full Employment Plan.

As we learned in 2008, it worked very well for the Wall Street Robber Barons. They "diversified" worker investments so well that, when the accounting was finally done, the funds had been distributed so cleverly, even the accountants had a hard time finding them. As a result, lawyers grabbed lots of fuel for their paper mills. In the end, ERISA probably was the Accountants and Lawyers and Wall Street Robber Barons Full Employment Act.

What it wasn't was a meaningful part of the vast majority of Boomers' retirement expectations, except if those expectations included endless working, scrimping and saving to ensure that the remaining Greediest (Brokaw's mindlessly lionized chosen cohort), and younger Greediest wannabes (such as stock brokers) kept their homes, yacht, health and futures.

Nor were IRAs alone affected. Employed Boomers, seeing the writing on the wall regarding Social Security and feeling the unease of working for companies suddenly unwilling to provide for them as they had provided for the Greediest, took advantage of 401(k)s when they could. When the crash came, the losses were frightful, compounded by the fact that companies could find ways to delay liquidation until it suited them, often after a distribution of their management fees.

One other thing was certain; investment companies were making lots of moola off those "defined contributions" whether the stocks rose or fell. The defined contributions meant that they, at least, could predict what sort of income they would have to "play with" over time.

It isn't easy being broke, but sometimes there's a bright side

The only bright spot, and it's a laughable one, is that so few Boomers were able to take advantage of IRAs and Keoghs.

About 50% of Americans earn less than $33,000. That's barely enough for a family to live on, never mind save major amounts from. And if they do save, it will be too little. Banks are paying virtually no interest; what you save today is pretty much, at current rates, what you'll be able to draw in ten or twenty years. It might be even less if inflation rises or the government devalues the money, or both.

If an American worker has any extra money, there's little choice but to put it into a stock-based IRA. Since the debacle of 2008, most banks are controlled by or at the very least in bed with the very stock brokerages that took the Dow to new lows, a boon for big investors, of course, who simply bought things up cheap, knowing the "little guy" would have to get back in sooner or later (and rich folks can wait, unlike poor ones) and drive prices up again.

The banks and brokerages are the only winners in the United States Mega-Disaster Lottery. The lottery ticket buyers — IRA owners, 401(k) participants — have nothing to gain by playing, and everything to lose. But they also lose in savings accounts held at miniscule interest rates, and they lose keeping it under the mattress. At some level, most people know when they are in a hopeless situation.

A good contention would be that savings rates are low in the US because the population, for all its touted ignorance, knows when it is throwing good money after bad and would rather have pleasure now since it's axiomatic — in the post-Reagan retirement sweepstakes — that they won't have any later no matter what they do. Sometimes — in the United States at present — profligacy is the only reasonable response to the admonition to save for a rainy day. The deluge had come, and those who can are swimming upstream as hard as they can.

Others are drowning. But all have realized spending money on some fun or comfort now beats giving more to the very people who've robbed you, the Greediest and the banker-Greediest-wannabes.

What the banks and brokers don't get, the government will

Nor was that the extent of the depredations legalized by ERISA. ERISA "allowed companies to reduce promised pension benefits by the equivalent of most of a worker's Social Security check" according to an article by David Cay Johnston in *Mother Jones (2010)*.

Before ERISA, a secretary who had a DB pension that would pay her $1,000 a month upon her retirement would get her full Social Security check, as well. Johnston uses the figure $732. So, in retirement, she would have $1,732 in income each month. After ERISA, her employer could reduce her company pension to $400, giving her $1132 each month. That held true until 1986, when the law was changed so that only "half a pension can be taken away via the Social Security offset." Big whoop; now the secretary will get $1,232, still a big difference from $1,732, and likely not enough to live on. That small gift was from Ronald Reagan's government, a sort of trickle down no doubt extracted as a beneficence from CEOs who had just seen their top marginal tax rate drop from 70 to 28 percent.

Lest we forget: In 1974, most CEOs and owners of businesses large enough to offer pension plans were The Greediest, not Boomers. In 1974, Congress was virtually all the Greediest.

In 1983, most CEOs and owners of businesses large enough to

offer pension plans were the Greediest, not Boomers. In 1983, Congress was still virtually all the Greediest.

Still more worrisome erosion of retirement benefits for Boomers

Until ERISA, pensions were required to invest in high-quality safe corporate bonds; little investment was permitted in more volatile instruments, such as stocks. That was helpful to the companies providing the pensions; the investments might not grow wildly, but neither would they tank. This assured both pension-plan managers and the pension recipients that, barring the dissolution of the company, they would get their pension as expected.

In 1974, however, Congress allowed pension fund managers to follow a "prudent man" principle; they merely had to look at what other fund managers were investing in and follow suit. (Apparently, Congress had never heard the phrase, "If all the other kids were jumping off the Brooklyn Bridge, would you want to do it too?") This was, needless to say, a wonderful boon for the stock market.

The good part of ERISA, if any, was that it was created in response to the loss of pensions by workers at Studebaker, which had gone belly up in 1964, costing about 2,900 union workers their retirement funds. Part of ERISA, in response to the first big retirement meltdown, was the Pension Benefit Guaranty Corporation (PBGC), an FDIC-like organization that protects pensions if a company fails. Theoretically. In fact, a misleadingly named act, the 2006 Pension Protection Act, allows companies to convert their DC single-employer plans to multi-employer plans.

So what? A lot. It also changed the government guarantee from $1,000 per week to $250. (Jones 2010) The bill was sponsored by Rep. John Boehner (R-Ohio), who was born in 1949. One would have thought a Boehner, as a Boomer, would have protected pensions from such risks, considering that he is within ten years of retirement himself. However, his ties to the financial markets and to industrial companies are strong, stronger obviously than his ties to Boomer well-being. A quick look at his sources of funding make that conclusion inescapable. His biggest recent contributor, according to OpenSecrets.org, is American Financial Group. Other large donors include:

American Electric Power, Lockheed Martin, US Bancorp, Blue Cross/Blue Shield, AT&T Inc, Chevron Corp, Financial Services Roundtable, Metlife Inc, National Assn of Health Underwriters, Nat'l Assn Real Estate Investment Trusts.

Note: The donations were not from the company itself, but from its PAC if any, individual members or employees or owners and the immediate families of those people.

What was Boehner thinking by making it even less possible for his own generation to enjoy their lives in retirement? Who knows. However, as a long-term member of Congress, it's not something he will personally have to worry about. In 2001, Paul Sperry, writing on WorldNetDaily.com, notes that unlike America's big losers of 2008—that is, anyone depending on a 401(k) for retirement funding — Congress "can't lose their gold-plated retirement plans."(Sperry 2009)

What makes them gold-plated? First, the amount they receive is based on an average of the highest paid three years, so the peak years are the basis. In addition, pension payments rise each year under a cost-of-living adjustment, or COLA, matching the Consumer Price Index rise. Almost no private pensions do that.

In addition, Sperry notes, lawmakers and their staffs can retire after 20 years' service as early as age 50; the rest of the nation must wait until age 65 for full benefits, such as they are, from their sole government pension, Social Security. Baby Boomers must wait longer. The minimum age for full retirement rises each year for the Baby Boom.

(This is in contrast to France, where, in September 2010, workers were up in arms because the government planned to raise the retirement age from 60 to 62 for full benefits. This on top of having, for one's entire working life, a month of vacation each year regardless of seniority, and what is generally regarded as the world's finest universal health care system. When a person retires in France, it is likely they won't be used up, worn out and discarded, in total contrast to the lot of most American workers.)

In addition, Congress also has a tax-deferred savings plan, matched by taxpayers almost dollar for dollar, plus Social Security benefits; like all workers, members of Congress pay into the system for the first $80,000 or so of their gross income, subject to change, of course, at the whim of Congress and the IRS.

Sperry (2010) noted that in the US: "Fewer than four out of 10 workers even have a pension, guaranteed or not. And the average worker with a pension qualifies for about a third of his or her pay, or about $7,500 a year – and that's fixed for life."

However, even most criminal misdeeds fail to poke holes in the golden parachutes of Congress. Sperry (2010) offers the case of "retired crook Dan Rostenkowski. After 36 years in the House, benefits for the former Ways and Means Committee chairman start at $96,462 a year, even though he was convicted of embezzling his office stamp allowance. (Only treason can strip federal lawmakers of their pension.)"

If an individual who has paid his or her FICA taxes for decades is convicted of a crime and sent to jail after age 65 (or whatever age benefits kick in for that birth year's retirees), Social Security payments will be withheld. Prisoners see this as unfair; they have paid into the system, after all, and now think they should get something out. The problem is, of course, they have not paid into it in the way they think. Their Social Security payments are not theirs; they do not own them. That is because it is not an investment or banking system; it is a wealth transfer system. What I pay in today will be used to pay my mother's check tomorrow. What my children pay in tomorrow will be used to pay my check the day after.

But wait: Boomers don't have many children. What then?

Good question, especially now that the Greediest have put our individual retirement savings on the skids.

Tone-deaf Boomers fail to heed IRA Epic Fail warning bell

In the spring of 2007, the National Bureau of Economic Research (NBER) (2009) issued a report that should have been a resounding gong to the ears of Baby Boomers approaching retirement, but apparently was not. Baby Boomers, as much as other segments of the society, were caught in the crash landing of the stock market with no parachutes deployed. The problem is that in some cases, the Baby Boomers could not do anything about altering the instruments their pension funds were invested in; in other cases, they were simply not savvy enough investors or politicians to heed the warning signals that their nest eggs were about to be eaten by large, rapacious birds, that is, the derivative manipulators of a greedy Wall Street (with my apologies for the redundancies.)

That same report noted that, "Over the past two decades, there has been a striking shift in employer-provided pensions from defined benefit (DB) to defined contribution (DC) plans. In a DB plan, a worker's benefit is determined by his work history and the specifics of his employer's plan, while in a DC plan, a worker's benefit is determined by his own and his employer's contributions and by asset returns."(NBEC 2009)

There are minimal variables for the employee in a DB plan. In fact, they are often limited to the length of time he or she has been with the company, and the level of the employee's job.

In DC plans, employees are facing all the same risks as anyone buying stocks and bonds, or worse, because it is not investment money — "fun money," or extra money — the employees are investing, it is the money with which they will need to fund their old age. All their retirement income is subject to market risk. "Investing" in a 401(k), then, is not so much investing but gambling.

Those who invest for reasons other than retirement income can afford risk; who cares if one buys that yacht this year or next, or never? But each of us must pay for our old age because the government's program is minimal, as it was meant to be, and employers — those same people whose profits were made with their employees' work — have been released from providing anything at all for those same people.

An NBER working paper compared results for workers in DC and DB plans, and concluded that, in the sort of robust market that existed when they did the study, those at the higher end of the earnings scale did slightly better in a DC plan than those in a DB plan. They noted, "However, when the authors reduce the rate of return on corporate stock by 300 basis points to allow for the possibility that future returns may be lower than past returns, DB and DC wealth values are much closer." (NBEC 2009)

Those "basis points" are analogous to Dow Jones numbers. In 2008, there was a reduction of a lot more than 300 "basis points" in the Dow Jones. Not only that, but it was a very rapid drop; even some people working in the financial sector had experienced significant losses before they realized the time had come to pull their money out of the volatile and all-but-ruined United States stock market and put the remainder in something safer, such as coins in the sock drawer.

The NBER study's authors noted that their analysis was simplified, ignoring the fact that employees often withdraw balances as lump sums when changing jobs, further reducing their wealth at retirement. The length of the employee's career was also ignored as were the precise mechanisms by which money was added to the DC plans. The authors themselves noted that further insight on those issues was "essential for understanding the long-run effect of the ongoing transition from DB to DC pension plans." (NBEC 2009)

Another major failure of the study, making it virtually worthless, is that employees were "assumed to invest in three assets —corporate stock, nominal long-term government bonds, and inflation-indexed long-term bonds (TIPS),"(NBED 2009) another imaginary occurrence.

In the end, it would be reasonable to ask why such a study was conducted at all. In the aftermath of the Bush Financial Meltdown of 2008, it is at least not difficult to find answers to how things got so bad just when the Baby Boom was set to begin retiring, or who was responsible.

One would have to ask what benefit there was in ERISA for Baby Boomers, and one would have to answer: None.

The sad fate of Social Security: It isn't what you think

John C. Goodman, president of the National Center for Policy Analysis, testified before Congress in 2005 concerning the bleak picture for Boomer retirement. He said:

> In the United States, we have made promises to senior citizens that far exceed what we can pay for at current tax rates. As a result, future retirees will have to rely more on private savings than previous generations. For this reason, we need programs that encourage private sector saving. The ideal would be to encourage private saving and reduce future government entitlement obligations at the same time. This could be accomplished with personal retirement accounts. (Goodman 2010)

There is one problem with this, of course. Most of the Baby Boomers haven't got enough time to benefit much from "private sector" — that is, their own — savings. Nor from such 401(k) investing as they can manage to do well.

Social Security is a pay-as-you-go system. Cash flow into the system must be greater than out of it, or a deficit results. In the early 2000s, both Social Security and Medicare spent more than they took in, getting a bailout from general government revenues of about $45 billion, Goodman said. He noted as well that the common belief that Social Security and Medicare are sound financially is also bankrupt:

> In fact, the latest numbers from the Trustees of Social Security and Medicare are staggering. In 2010, the federal government will need $127 billion in additional funds to pay promised benefits. Five years later, the size of the annual deficit will double. Five years beyond that, it will double again. In just 15 years, the federal government will have to raise taxes, reduce other spending or borrow $761 billion to keep its promises to America's senior citizens.(Goodman 2010)

In short, the early Baby Boomers will either be an enormous burden on their already strapped offspring, or they will do without. In some ways, it is not difficult to see how the generally humane Boomers have become so frightened of euthanasia by government fiat, especially with imbecilic politicians like Sarah Palin and Michele Bachmann stirring the pot.

But it is the Silent Generation, which comprises the majority of the morally bankrupt Teabagger movement, who are most frightened — so frightened that they often claim to be Boomers even when they clearly are not. If one extrapolates and argues that Fox News is the cable news network of choice for Teabaggers, it is clear that they are NOT Boomers; they are Silent Generation. An August, 2010 report noted that the average age of Fox News viewers was 65, and the report added, "its viewers are even older than viewers of Hallmark Channel, Military Channel and Golf Channel."(Hibberd 2010)

Note well: **NO BOOMER WAS 65 in AUGUST, 2010.** The oldest, from the smallest year of the Baby Boom, was barely 64. The majority of Boomers had not yet reached 60.

> The Greediest had it made in the shade while Boomers bit it big-time. "The oldest Americans endured last year [2009] better than their younger counterparts. Those 65 and above saw a substantial increase in real median income, up 5.8% for the group." (Dougherty 2010)

By 2020, Goodman notes, it will require one of every two tax dollars each year to fund Social Security and Medicare. The amounts are so staggering, it's ridiculous even to attempt to understand them. But that's all right. As it happens, it's all pie-in-the-sky anyway. There is no real money in the Social Security and Medicare Trust Funds. The "funds" merely serve an accounting function. When the taxes taken in exceed payments out, the government creates special bonds to hold the funds. But they aren't real bonds; they cannot be sold in the marketplace like municipal bonds and so on. Indeed, they are just paper creations held in filing cabinets in Parkersburg, WVA. Medicare bonds aren't even on paper, but only on computers. The so-called bonds have no actual value, although when taxes fall short of needs, the "bonds" are removed from the cabinets or computer. Where do they go? The trash bin. In essence, the "bonds" are no more than IOUs the government has written to itself.

To repeat: Social Security/Medicare bonds are valueless. Worse, they barely exist, even in cyberspace. How hard would it be for politicians of the future — or even John Boehner in the present — to conveniently forget about them completely?

Goodman compares the entire process to chain letters, and says that approach to paying for retirement benefits must come to an end.

Fine. But who is going to suffer the birth pangs of another system? Whose benefits will be cut? Guess.

Social Security time-bomb set to blast the Boomers

When Franklin D. Roosevelt's New Deal set up the Social Security system, it was for several reasons. There were many new old poor people because of the stock market crash, and humanitarian concerns suggested not letting them starve on the streets. Plus, a war was looming; young men would go off to fight, and then who would take care of extended families?

If there had ever been any discussion of changing the method by which Social Security was funded, they were doubtless left on the table and forgotten as the returning soldiers began to marry and start farm-size families without the farms. There would be lots of people to pay the freight on the old soldiers. And there the thinking stopped. Who would pay the freight for the children of the old soldiers, the Baby Boom? All of a sudden, in the aftermath of the Bush financial crash, the problem of saddling future generations with burdensome debt is arising; why did it never arise during the 1960s, 1970s and even 1980s?

Because the time-bombs that would destroy the Baby Boom were dirty little secrets the architects and beneficiaries of post-WWII fiscal policy and political maneuvering didn't want anyone to know about, much less think about. In short, it was not in the Greediests' best interest to tell the truth, so of course, that settled the matter.

In the 1960s, the Greediest were on top of the world and thought only about how to stay there. Among their maneuvers were shifting college costs from parent to student, and inventing the universal credit card so Boomers could buy ever more "stuff" to keep the military-industrial complex that was supporting the Greediest rolling.

In the 1970s, the Baby Boom had Vietnam to worry about, and finding a job in a contracting economy, a project that was difficult despite their education. They had to compete for those jobs, wildly, unlike their parents who waltzed into ready-made jobs after WWII.

In the 1980s, there was Reagan, yapping on about his "Star Wars" project to protect us from a down-and-out Soviet Union and its anemic remaining threat and using his "Great Communicator" skills to convince the Baby Boom that if we just let him take care of the upper classes, the bounty would trickle down to us. And it did...because liquid waste will flow downhill. In fact, it didn't trickle down. It rolled down from the heights on which the Greediest sat to spread itself out in every conceivable space, every area of the lives of the Baby Boom.

A retirement system in which government cannot rob you

A funded retirement system, in which worker contributions are invested and with each worker's contributions accruing only to that worker, is the way 30 other nations have transformed their systems from chain-letter style to partially or fully funded systems. The contributions are not voluntary, any more than Social Security/FICA contributions are voluntary. The difference is accountability by government. In those nations, government cannot rob Peter to pay Paul, nor shift one generation's burden to another. There is choice for the worker among various vehicles. But perhaps best of all for the worker, and worst of all for politicians, such personal retirement accounts create a "check on government power" because of the ownership rights inherent in the program, Goodman says.

That is, of course, why it has consistently failed. Politicians depend on manipulating retired and about to retire constituents to get re-elected. It saves them doing any meaningful work. And it allows them to enhance or destroy the prospects of any given generation at will.

Worst among the offenders is that well-trained Baby Boomer, Rep. John Boehner (R-OH), who exemplifies the transfer of the WWII ethic to a once-very-different generation.

If there is no downside for throwback politicians like Boehner for standing in the way of pension reform, then there is absolute profit in stripping constituents of existing pensions, as was done via the 2006 Pension Protection Act. (It might be worthwhile learning to read the names of Congressional bills as one would read personal ads. In a personal ad, "a few extra pounds" generally means flabby. In Congressional bills, "protection" generally means the population is about to be screwed.)

For Boehner, and others like him, there's no downside to stripping their constituents of pensions to enrich corporations. Constituents don't offer junkets or make large campaign donations that allow Congress to buy advertising to entice constituents to vote the into office again and again. Because most constituents don't read the Congressional Record regularly, most don't know when someone like Boehner dilutes pension laws protecting individuals. Even if they knew, until the Internet, constituents had precious little hope of getting their knowledge to others, and even now, it's difficult. It's much more difficult than using financial sector largesse to buy advertising that reaches millions, as the representatives can do.

All a member of Congress or the Senate has to do is get re-elected for 20 years, and then the Congressional golden parachute will protect them from all the vagaries of financial life that beset the nation, no matter how well or how badly they served their constituencies in the meantime.

Sperry suggests a cure:

> Denying lawmakers their lavish taxpayer-subsidized pensions would go a long way toward discouraging them from treating election to public office as a career rather than a chance to serve their nation. It would also curb the pork-barrel spending that nourishes incumbency.(Sperry 2009)

If they had to retire on the economy like the rest of us, it would also inhibit their zeal for laws that transfer the fruits of individual labors to the coffers of corporations. Their 40s(k) would be as likely to tank as mine or yours.

What sort of impetus could be used to get them to reform the way Social Security and Medicare are funded escapes me. They would be likely to participate in any such change. And such a change would eliminate some of their power over the retired and soon-to-retire among their constituents, it would seem they have a negative reinforcer for creating a funded retirement program.

That's probably why they haven't done it. And why they won't.

To repeat: Congress is *still* primarily the Greediest and the Silent Generation. Such few Boomers as there in Congress are very often are cut from the same traditional cloth as John Boehner, a carbon-copy of the patronizing Congress members of a former time, the Greediest time in US history.

No matter where you live, or what election is coming up — school board, local, state, national —
It's time to vote them out.

CONCLUSION

This book is by no means exhaustive. It has located and followed some of the trails to where Boomers find themselves today, as a reviled generation, looked down up by its elders, castigated for louts by younger cohorts.

This work has attempted to explain how blame for the current societal and financial — not to mention military — distress belongs only in very small part to the Boomers, and much more substantially to Tom Brokaw's illicitly lionized cohort, the people he calls the Greatest Generation, but whose conduct was anything but saintly, from WWII to the present. Brokaw's elevation of a very ordinary, and some would claim substandard, generation to such a lofty pedestal was inexcusable as journalism, reprehensible as a self-serving exercise in making fame into fortune at the expense of several generations of Americans. (For a much more balance, and well-researched, portrait of Brokaw's chosen generation, visit: http://www.vqronline.org/articles/2002/winter/duke-greatest-generation/ .)

Indeed, the elevation itself all but spelled misery for the Baby Boom generation. It was not bad enough that we had been trashed for traitors if we, as young draft-susceptible students, protested Vietnam. We were trashed for warmongers if our personal ethos demanded that we serve. The GI Generation profited by splitting us; they feared our power in sheer numbers if we were not at each other's throats, and it is to their benefit to keep it that way today, to ally with younger generations to make it seem that every rotten thing is the Boomers' doing when only a small part of it is.

There has been, therefore, no consistency across the Boomer generation as there had been in WWII. Despite the nation's original unwillingness to enter that war, once it was done, it became universally patriotic to serve or if not serve, support the war effort. How FDR managed that is quite clever, considering the still rampant dislike of Jews in the United States at the time, and the knowledge that, to some point at least, our entry into that war was about saving Jewish lives.

To the ordinary grunt, it was more about helping one of our allies, England. France: Not so much. Despite the effective Resistance in France, the French never earned much more than US disdain for their efforts. Because Americans are circumscribed by their inability to admire foreign languages? It's hard to know, but what's easy to see is that disdain for the French was transmitted from the GI Generation to the Boomers and beyond; recall the "freedom fries" when the French refused to follow the US and the UK into the never-ending war games in Afghanistan and Iraq. One might easily ask, who's sorry now?

Indeed, the US is. Because of the Star Wars mentality brought to the US presidency by cowboy/actor Ronald Reagan, it was easy enough for his ideological offspring, acting cowboy George W. Bush, to export mayhem. Unfortunately, Bush was a least son, unable to do even that very well. And unfortunately, chronologically, he's a member of the Baby Boom.

That did not do the Boomer generation any good. Nor do the other outspoken standard bearers for the most broken of the nation's promises, politicians like John Boehner, for example. The worldview of the Dubyas and Boehners was a tired one when their fathers lived in it and passed it on. It is now exhausted, and needs to be planted six feet under. The ideas of these unregenerate throwbacks are not those of the true Baby

Boom, the generation that protested war successfully, worked with the leading lights of the Silent Generation, mainly, for equality, and made Earth Day into a meaningful event that changed our relationship with our planet, at least until Dubya tossed his garbage into the mix.

While the Baby Boom is not monolithically liberal or progressive, it is the generation that by and large refused the knee-jerk conservatism of unfettered capitalism, that desired a more compassionate approach to government, a more humanitarian approach to solving social problems. Indeed, even recognizing social problems was not something many of the GI Generation engaged in. The few who did — the Rev. Martin Luther King, Bobby Kennedy, and more — were often killed for their trouble. Boomers went to jail demonstrating on behalf of fairness and justice time after time, and news reports at the end of September 2010 indicated a new government juggernaut to investigate any student with ties to such "subversive" organizations as Students for a Democratic Society (SDS), just like in the old days. Only this time, it is Boomer's kids who are under the microscope and under the federal investigative gun.

In addition to being jailed (as Boomer journalist Amy Goodman was during the run up to Mr. Obama's election in September 2008), Boomers were killed for their trouble. Kent State was one of the biggest travesties of government intervention in a peaceable demonstration in US history, carried out under the ignominious administration of a most unlikeable GI Generation Greeder, Richard M. Nixon.

It is time the rest of the world noticed that the Boomers are still, by and large, not their father's children. They are the generation that changed so much about modern life that the Xes and Ys and Joneses find good, but fail to credit to the Boomers. Boomers are the generation whose activist powers are claimed so often, these days, by teabaggers, a sorrier excuse for Boomerdom than has ever before been seen. Make no mistake: in 2010, the oldest Boomer is not collecting full Social Security because that Boomer is only 64 years old. No Boomer could claim to be a bagger because they feared their current Social Security would be reduced; No Boomer was on full Social Security, except perhaps via disability for a few.

Just for Boomers — and because they had already claimed so much for themselves — the Greediest Generation pushed up the age for receiving full benefits to 66. Some will say it's to keep Social Security solvent. Yes, perhaps. But it is also to ensure than no one currently on Social Security need give up one red cent, not even so that their children may live, not so their children's children may live.

Boomers are not perfect. Neither are they the greedy demons Boomer bashers have been screeching about. Indeed, the Boomer generation has suffered more, and will continue to suffer more, from the fallout of the 2008 financial meltdown than any other generational cohort. Only the Boomers have yet to begin collecting Social Security while having insufficient time to build up anything else to compensate. Why didn't they do it before now? Boomer bashing often hinges on that fact, that the Boomers haven't saved. Why? Flat wages. Plus Boomers have been sandwiched between whining parents and needful children. They've been whacked by Greeder government policies regarding immigration, housing, food and education. Boomers did the best they could under the circumstances. With luck, Xers and Ys and Joneses will be able to climb out, as they still have some time. But they must understand: it is not the Boomers who put them there. It is the Greeders.

The Greeders did the best they could, but only for themselves. When they wanted to make more money in the stock market, it was easy. Just ramp up corporate profits. How? Shift the pension burden from the corporation to the individual. When? Just at the time Boomers have been working a few years and are ready to be vested in the retirement plan. And grandfather the benefits for the Greeders.

There is only one option left to the Baby Boom as I see it; stop protecting our greedy elders, and start helping the younger generations understand the burden the Greeders placed on Boomers, Xers, Ys and Joneses. Spend not one cent we don't need to on anything that will not help our own or subsequent generations.

Is this a call, then, for abandoning those already retired, the remaining Greeders and Silent Generation?

In a word, yes. They've pretty much grabbed everything they need in any case, but that doesn't mean they don't want more. Test it if you like, but it would be my guess that, asked to contribute so much as ten dollars a week to a fund to help Boomers rebuild their own retirement accounts, the volume of the HELL NO that proceeded from Greeder throats would blow masts off tall buildings. Ask them to contribute to keep Xers and Ys and Joneses employed, and those masts would come tumbling down.

Would all of the Greeders refuse to help? Probably not. Just the great bulk of them living it up in Florida and Arizona, crying about their sudden inability to take three grand vacations this year, and sporting the Greeders' favorite bumper sticker, "Out spending my grandchildren's inheritance" on the back of the gas guzzling land yachts they cruise around in like so many white-haired GIs home on leave.

WORKS CITED

Altschuler, Glenn C., and Stuart M. Blumin. *The G.I. Bill: A New Deal for Veterans*. Oxford: Oxford UP, 2009: 7.

"Baby Boomers' Unhappy Future." *Washington Times* [Washington, DC] 26 Dec. 2005: A17.

Barr, John. "Report Urges Oversight of Binghamton University Athletic Department - ESPN." *ESPN: The Worldwide Leader In Sports*. Web. 09 Sept. 2010. <http://sports.espn.go.com/ncb/news/story?id=4906365>.

Bennet, James. "How the Cleaver Family Destroyed Our S&Ls; Low Mortgages, High CD Rates and Money Market Funds Allowed Americans over 40 to Take the Rest of Us to the Cleaners." *Washington Monthly* Sept. 1990: 38+.

Bohan, Suzanne. "Bohemian Grove Exposed." *Alex Jones' Prison Planet.com*. 2 Aug. 1999. Web. 09 Sept. 2010. <http://www.prisonplanet.com/world_leaders_engage_i n_symbolic_pagan_worship.html>.

Bowen, Kevin. "Credit Counseling - Effective for Bankruptcy? GreenshieldFS.com." *Debt Relief - Debt Help GreenshieldFS.com*. 5 Jan. 2010. Web. 09 Sept. 2010. <http://www.greenshieldfs.com/understanding-financial-health/articles/credit-counseling/credit-counseling-effective-bankruptcy>.

Clark, Robert L, Richard V Burkhauser, and Marilyn Moon. *The Economics of an Aging Society*. New York: Wiley-Blackwell, 2004: 80.

Cockburn, Alexander. "Corporate Interests Keep World's Poor Hungry". *Business Post* June 29, 2003: http://archives.tcm.ie/businesspost/2003/06/29/story90970 1237.asp

" 'Conservatives' Are Single-Largest Ideological Group". Gallup. Fall, 2010

<http://www.gallup.com/poll/120857/conservatives-single-largest-ideological-group.aspx>.

"CSPAN booknotes (1999)". brothers judd. Spring, 2009
<http://brothersjudd.com/index.cfm/fuseaction/reviews.d
etail/book_id/170/Greatest%20Gen.htm>.

Daniel, Pete. "The USDA Legacy: From the New Deal to Silent
Spring ". Historical Text Archive. Spring, 2009
<http://historicaltextarchive.com/sections.php?action=rea
d&artid=656>. (Quoting L. C. Salter to Ezra Taft Benson,
November 2, 1953; Wilbert McReynolds to Ezra Taft
Benson, January 26, 1953, farm program, Records of the
Secretary of Agriculture, Record Group 16, National
Archives and Records Administration.)

Der Hovanesian, Mara. "USDA Home Loans: Subprime
Redux?" *Business Week*. Winter, 2010
<http://www.businessweek.com/magazine/content/09_39
/b4148028475445.htm>.

Dougherty, Conor. "Lost Decade for American Income."
Business News & Financial News - *The Wall Street Journal*
- WSJ.com. Wall Street Journal, 17 Sept. 2010. Web. 18
Sept. 2010.
<http://online.wsj.com/article/SB100014240527487034406 0
4575495670714069694.html>.

Dreher, Rod. "USDA-Disapproved: Small Farmers and Big
Government". *National Review*, January 27, 2003.

Dunsky, Robert M., and James R. Follain. "Tax-Induced
Portfolio Reshuffling: The Case of the Mortgage Interest
Deduction.(Statistical Data Included)." *Real Estate
Economics* (2000). *Access My Library*. Web. 9 Sept. 2010.
<http://www.accessmylibrary.com/article-1G1-
70739736/tax-induced-portfolio-reshuffling.html>.

Dutch, Steven. "Killing the Messenger: Attacks on the SAT".
July, 2010 <
http://www.uwgb.edu/dutchs/pseudosc/denysat.htm>.

Fredrix, Emily. "Corn Syrup Producers Want Sweeter Name: Corn Sugar." *The Huffington Post*. 14 Sept. 2010. Web. 14 Sept. 2010. <http://www.huffingtonpost.com/huff-wires/20100914/us-corn-syrup-image/>.

Friedman, Mark. "Baby Boomers slow to save for retirement: 'Greatest Generation' comes to rescue, again.(Wealth Management)." Arkansas Business. Journal Publishing, Inc. 2006. 7 Sep. 2009

Goodman, John C. "Baby Boomer Retirement: The Nightmare in our Future". National Center for Policy Analysis. Winter, 2010 <http://www.ncpa.org/speech/baby-Boomer-retirement-the-nightmare-in-our-future>.

Granered, Erik. *Global Call Centers: Achieving Outstanding Customer Service across Cultures & Time Zones*. Boston: Nicholas Brealey International, 2005: 18.

Halweil, Brian. "Where have all the farmers gone?". *World Watch*, September 2000: 12-12.

Hibberd, James. "Average Age of the Fox News viewer: 65". Democratic Underground. Sept. 7, 2010 <http://www.democraticunderground.com/discuss/duboard.php?az=view_all&address=389x8923510>.

Hira, Ron, and Anil Hira. *Outsourcing America: What's behind Our National Crisis and How We Can Reclaim American Jobs*. New York: American Management Association, 2005:3.

Historical Reference Directory Volume 2A, "Speech by General William C. Westmoreland before the Third Annual Reunion of the Vietnam Helicopter Pilots Association, July 5, 1986". Vietnam Helicopter Flight Crew Network. Spring, 2009 <http://www.vhfcn.org/stat.html#WESTY>.

Homan, Timothy R. "America's Wealthy Save Tax Cuts Rather Than Spend, Moody's Says - BusinessWeek." Editorial. *Businessweek* 14 Sept. 2010. *BusinessWeek - Business News,*

Stock Market & Financial Advice. Businessweek, 14 Sept. 2010. Web. 14 Sept. 2010. <http://www.businessweek.com/news/2010-09-14/america-s-wealthy-save-tax-cuts-rather-than-spend-moody-s-says.html>.

Ibrahim, Darian M. "A Return to Descartes: Property, Profit, and the Corporate Ownership of Animals". *Law and Contemporary Problems* 2007: 89+.

Jones, David Cay. "Pension Privateers." *Mother Jones*. Winter, 2010 <http://motherjones.com/politics/2009/05/who-ran-away-your-401k>.

Kochan, Thomas. "Wages and the Social Contract." Editorial. *The American Prospect* 22 Apr. 2007. *Home | The American Prospect*. 22 Apr. 2007. Web. 09 Sept. 2010. <http://www.prospect.org/cs/articles?article=wages_and_the_social_contract>

Kohn, Alfie. "NCLB: 'Too Destructive To Salvage'" CommonDreams.org." *Common Dreams - News & Views*. USA Today, 31 May 2007. Web. 09 Sept. 2010. <http://www.commondreams.org/archive/2007/05/31/1558>.

Levinson, Meridith. "Unemployment Hammers Younger Workers". *CIO* magazine. Summer, 2009 <http://www.ncpa.org/speech/baby-Boomer-retirement-the-nightmare-in-our-future>.

Lhotska, Lida. "Main:illness_and_medical_bills_cause_half_of_all_bank ruptcies [Politics of Health]." *Politics of Health Knowledge Network*. Physicians for a National Health Program, 5 Feb. 2005. Web. 09 Sept. 2010. <http://www.politicsofhealth.org/main/illness_and_medi cal_bills_cause_half_of_all_bankruptcies>.

Madden, Russell. "The Greatest Generation." Web. 10 Sept. 2010.

<http://home.earthlink.net/~rdmadden/webdocs/Greatest
_Generation.html>.

Mamatas, Nick. "The Term Paper Artist". Drexel University.
Sept. 6, 2010
<http://www.thesmartset.com/article/article10100801.asp
x>.

McBride, Laura H. "Republican Tortures for the American
Middle Class: The Warren Burger Supreme Court -
Washington DC Ethical Issues | Examiner.com."
Examiner.com. 3 Apr. 2009. Web. 09 Sept. 2010.
<http://www.examiner.com/ethical-issues-in-
washington-dc/republican-tortures-for-the-american-
middle-class-the-warren-burger-supreme-court>.

McCaffrey, Lt. Gen. Barry M. "Speech by Lt. Gen. Barry R.
McCaffrey, Memorial Day 1993". Vietnam Helicopter
Flight Crew Network. Spring, 2009 <www.vhfcn.org>.

McKinley, James C. "Texas Conservatives Win Curriculum
Change." The New York Times - Breaking News, World
News & Multimedia. New York Times, 12 Mar. 2010.
Web. 23 Sept. 2010.
<http://www.nytimes.com/2010/03/13/education/13texas.
html>.

"Medical Bills Leading Cause of Bankruptcy, Harvard Study
Finds." ConsumerAffairs.com: Knowledge Is Power!
Consumer News, Reviews, Complaints, Resources,
Safety Recalls. Feb. 2005. Web. 09 Sept. 2010.
<http://www.consumeraffairs.com/news04/2005/bankrup
tcy_study.html>.

Mercola, Dr. Joseph. "America's Deadliest Sweetener Betrays
Millions, Then Hoodwinks You With Name Change".
Huffington Post. July 7, 2010
<http://www.huffingtonpost.com/dr-mercola/americas-
deadliest-sweete_b_630549.html>.

National Park Service, September 5, 2010: <http://www.u-s-history.com/pages/h1605.html>

Niskanen, William A. "Reaganomics, by William A. Niskanen: The Concise Encyclopedia of Economics." *Library of Economics and Liberty*. 2002. Web. 09 Sept. 2010. <http://www.econlib.org/library/Enc1/Reaganomics.html>.

Norris, Floyd. "Editorial Observer; Bankruptcy Reform That Spares the Wealthy." *New York Times*. 9 Apr. 1999. Web. 9 Sept. 2010. <http://www.nytimes.com/1999/05/09/opinion/editorial-observer-bankruptcy-reform-that-spares-the-wealthy.html>

Olson, Keith W. *The GI Bill, the Veterans and the Colleges*. Lexington: University Press of Kentucky , 1974: 109.

Peterson, James R. "Designer Mortgages: the Boom in Nontraditional Mortgage Loans May Be a Double-edged Sword. So Far, Most Banks Have Moved Cautiously. Banking & Finance Banking, Lending & Credit Services from AllBusiness.com." Small Business Advice from the Champions of Small Business. *ABA Banking Journal*, 1 Oct. 2005. Web. 09 Sept. 2010. <http://www.allbusiness.com/government/620334-1.html>.

Pogrebin, Robin. "Underground Mail Road". *New York Times*. March, 2010 <http://www.neutronmedia.com/article.html The New York Times>.

Reinberg, Steven. "Suicide Rates Rise Among Baby Boomers Middle-aged White Women at Increasing Risk, Study Finds." Editorial. *US News & World Report* 21 Oct. 2008. *Health News Articles - US News Health*. 21 Oct. 2008. Web. 10 Sept. 2010. <http://health.usnews.com/articles/health/healthday/2008/10/21/suicide-rates-rise-among-baby-Boomers.html>.

"Retirement Wealth in Defined Benefit and Defined
    Contribution Pension Plans". National Bureau for
    Economic Research.
    <http://www.nber.org/aginghealth/spring07/w12597.htm
    l> Winter, 2009

Rich, Motoko. "For the Unemployed Over 50, Fears of Never
    Working Again." *New York Times*. New York Times, 20
    Sept. 2110. Web. 21 Sept. 2010.
    <http://www.nytimes.com/2010/09/20/business/economy/
    20older.html?pagewanted=1&_r=1&hp>.

Rosnick, David. "The Wealth of the Baby Boom Cohorts After
    the Collapse of the Housing Bubble". Center for
    Economic and Policy Research. Winter, 2010
    <http://www.cepr.net/index.php/publications/reports/the
    -wealth-of-the-baby-Boom-cohorts-after-the-collapse-of-
    the-housing-bubble/>.

Sawyer, Gordon. *The Agribusiness Poultry Industry*, 1971. 176-
    177. Quoted by Ibrahim.

Schapsmeier, Edward L and Frederick H. "Eisenhower and
    Agricultural Reform: Ike's Farm Policy Legacy
    Appraised". *The American Journal of Economics and
    Sociology*, 51, April 1992: 147-159.

"Bohemian Grove Fact Sheet." Sonoma County Free Press -
    Peace, Justice, Sustainability for All. Sonoma County
    Free Press. Web. 23 Sept. 2010.
    <http://www.sonomacountyfreepress.com/bohos/bohofa
    ct.html>.

Sperry, Paul. "Congress' cushy pension system".
    WorldNetDaily. Winter, 2009
    <http://www.wnd.com/index.php?pageId=9971>.

"Statistics about the Vietnam War". Vietnam Helicopter Flight
    Crew Network. Spring, 2009
    <http://www.vhfcn.org/stat.html>.

"Student Loan Bankruptcy Exception." FinAid! Financial Aid, College Scholarships and Student Loans. Fin Aid Page, LLC. Web. 13 Sept. 2010. <http://www.finaid.org/questions/bankruptcyexception.phtml>.

"The Bush Administration's Dirty Legacy". National Resources Defense Council. Aug. 30, 2010 <http://www.nrdc.org/bushrecord/>.

Tichenor, Daniel J. *Dividing Lines: the Politics of Immigration Control in America.* Princeton, NJ: Princeton UP, 2002.: 177.

W. L. Popham to B. T. Shaw, January 12, 1960, regulatory crops, no. 253, Records of the Agricultural Research Service, Record Group 310, National Archives and Records Administration (Hereafter cited ARS Records, RG 310, NARA). R. A. Moncrief to David R. Obey, October 30, 1969, pesticides, box 5081, SOA, RG 16, NARA. For an overview of the use of chemicals in the post-World War II South, see Daniel, Lost Revolutions, 61-87. <http://historicaltextarchive.com/sections.php?action=read&artid=656>.

Wassel, Judith I. "Boomerang Burdens: Back to the Nest." *Aging Well Magazine.* 2008. Web. 09 Sept. 2010. <http://www.agingwellmag.com/archive/071708pb.shtml>.

"What's So Great About the Greatest Generation?". Spring, 2009 <http://12angrymen.wordpress.com/2007/03/27/whats-so-great-about-the-greatest-generation/>.

Whipps, Heather. "Boomers Seek 'Green' Death. LiveScience, accessed at http://www.livescience.com/environment/071130-green-deaths.html

White, Jane. "Work Until You're Dead? That May Be the Only Option for Many Americans". Huffington Post. Sept. 6,

2010 <http://www.huffingtonpost.com/jane-white/post_785_b_703802.html>.

Williamson, Brady C. "Bankruptcy Laws." *Encyclopedia.com*. 2003. Web. 9 Sept. 2010. <http://www.encyclopedia.com/doc/1G2-3401800367.html>.

Wolff, Richard D. "Rising Income Inequality in the US: Divisive, Depressing, and Dangerous" 4 Feb. 2010. Web. 09 Sept. 2010. <http://www.rdwolff.com/content/rising-income-inequality-us-divisive-depressing-and-dangerous>.

Yang, Philip Q. *Post-1965 Immigration to the United States: Structural Determinants*. Westport, CT: Praeger, 1995.: 18.

Yates, Judith. "Affordability and Access to Home Ownership: Past, Present and Future?" *National Research Venture 3: Housing Affordability for Lower Income Australians* (2007). Australian Housing and Urban Research Institute. Web. 6 Sept. 2010. <www.ahuri.edu.au/publications/download/nrv3_research_paper_10>.

Zaitchick, Alexander. "Is the Future Going Down the Drain? Baby Boomers Going Bust". AlterNet. Winter, 2010 <www.alternet.org/workplace/130361/is_the_future_going_down_the_drain_baby_Boomers_going_bust/?page=entire>.

Zinn, Howard. "The Greatest Generation? by Howard Zinn." Editorial. *The Progressive* Oct. 2001. Third World Traveler, Third World, United States Foreign Policy, Alternative Media, Travel. Web. 09 Sept. 2010. <http://www.thirdworldtraveler.com/Zinn/Greatest_Generation.html>.

www.ingramcontent.com/pod-product-compliance
Lightning Source LLC
Chambersburg PA
CBHW030429290526
45786CB00001B/207